LEEDS'S MILITARY LEGACY

PAUL CHRYSTAL

Pen & Sword
MILITARY

To the memory of Leeds's First World War munitions workers.

First published in Great Britain in 2017 by
PEN AND SWORD MILITARY
an imprint of
Pen and Sword Books Ltd
47 Church Street
Barnsley
South Yorkshire S70 2AS

ISBN 978 1 52670 766 6

Typeset by Aura Technology and Software Services, India
Printed and bound by CPI Group (UK) Ltd, Croydon, CR0 4YY

Pen & Sword Books Ltd incorporates the imprints of Pen & Sword
Archaeology, Atlas, Aviation, Battleground, Discovery, Family History, History, Maritime,
Military, Naval, Politics, Railways, Select, Social History, Transport, True Crime, Claymore Press,
Frontline Books, Leo Cooper, Praetorian Press, Remember When, Seaforth Publishing and Wharncliffe.

For a complete list of Pen and Sword titles please contact
Pen and Sword Books Limited
47 Church Street, Barnsley, South Yorkshire, S70 2AS, England
email: enquiries@pen-and-sword.co.uk
website: www.pen-and-sword.co.uk

CONTENTS

INTRODUCTION

Leeds has a rich and varied military heritage. This book charts that heritage from Roman times to the end of the Second World War.

There was clearly limited military activity after the Roman invasion of Britain and through the Anglo-Saxon periods. Decisive battles of the Wars of the Roses skirted Leeds to the south but, as a strategically important city, Leeds only came into its own in the English Civil War when it was a target for both Royalist and Parliamentarian armies. The city had a flirtation with the conflicts of the 18th-century Jacobite Uprisings and its regiments were mobilized in the industrial and social unrest caused by Chartism and Luddism.

Leeds responded enthusiastically in the call to arms for volunteer regiments in the 19th century amid fears of French invasion and French-style popular revolution. Some its most famous regiments find their origins at this time: Leeds Volunteers, Leeds Rifles and the 1st (Leeds) Yorkshire West Riding Artillery Volunteer Corps; 2nd West Yorkshire Royal Engineer Volunteers and the Yorkshire Hussars Yeomanry (Alexandra, Princess of Wales's Own). Local industry, not least brewers Joshua Tetley, supported this with a ready supply of horses and men.

The Second Boer War saw Leeds regiments serve with distinction, winning one VC. But it was in the First World War where Leeds men and women excelled themselves in patriotism and bravery and, sadly, sacrifice and slaughter. On the home front local industry and local men and women excelled in war-effort work: military uniforms were made in their tens of thousands while the heroines of the Barnbow munitions factory turned out even more munitions: thirty-seven of the Canary Girls and two men tragically died working for their country in three fateful explosions.

The Second World War was met by the people of Leeds with similar patriotism and fortitude, be it on the home front or on the front line. Industry boosted the war effort and regiments and an RAF squadron fought with distinction.

As a fitting epilogue we visit the remarkable Leeds Royal Armouries Museum, no better place to celebrate Leeds's glorious military heritage.

1. ROMAN, ANGLO-SAXON AND NORMAN MILITARY LEEDS

The place we now know as Leeds was of little, if any, military significance until the English Civil War in the 17th century. Before the Romans came in AD 43, and during the early part of their occupation at least, the region, Brigantia, was occupied by the Celtic tribe known as the Brigantes, the largest tribe in Britain in terms of territory. No doubt the Brigantes fought with neighbouring tribes to defend their territory against incursions, livestock raids and kidnappings; no doubt they responded in kind with raids over their borders into enemy territory. The Carvetii were to the north-west, the Parisii to the east and the Corieltauvi and the Cornovii to the south. To the north were the Votadini who settled the lands up to the present-day border between England and Scotland.

While of no strategic significance, the area around Leeds was settled by Bronze Age and Celtic peoples. Roman Bronze Age objects have been found, including two barrows on Woodhouse Moor. In the pre-Roman and Roman Iron Age, Brigantian earthworks and a possible Roman paved ford across the Aire at today's Leeds Bridge have been excavated. The Leeds historian Ralph Thoresby (1658–1725) cites evidence (now lost) of a Roman fort at Quarry Hill on the site of the West Yorkshire Playhouse but this remains doubtful, as does the suggestion that this was in fact Cambodunum, which is actually at Slack near Huddersfield. We are on safer ground with part of a Roman hypocaust (the underground heating system for a house or bath house) which was unearthed in the early 20th century in the sewage works that stood where the White Rose Centre is now. Roman coins and other small finds have been made on the Cardinals Estate and up Churwell Hill. Just east of Leeds Bridge, archaeological finds may suggest the presence of a *mansio*, one of the thousands of posting stations along the *cursus publicus* following the major road network of the Roman empire where riders rested and horses were watered, shoed, cared for by vets, stabled and passed on to the next dispatch rider.

Brigantian and Roman remains have also been found at Adel, a place of minor military strategic importance. Adel (Roman name Burgodunum) is near the site of a Roman fort on the Roman road from York to Ilkley via Tadcaster; five Roman-inscribed stones have been found there. The footpath by the side of Long Causeway was allegedly made from the original Roman stones, until removed by the council in the 1960s on the grounds of health and safety.

Of the five inscribed stones there are two altar stones dedicated to different goddesses, one found in 1879 at Church Lane, Chapel Allerton and now in the Leeds Museum; the other found in 1816 at Adel and now in the coach-house of Adel Church. The first is inscribed MΛTRIBVS ... ... M 'To the Mother [goddesses ... a vow absolved freely and] deservedly'; the second DEΛE BRIGAN D CINGETISSA P 'To the goddess Brigantia a dedication placed by Cingetissa'. The third is a building stone inscribed with a phallus found in the same year that carries the inscription PRIMINVS MENT[U]LA 'Priminus is a Prick'! The other two are fragments of two tombstones discovered in 1702 at Adel Mill; both are now lost. The inscriptions read: D M S CADIEDI NIAE FORTVNATAE PIA V A X ... 'To the holy shades of the departed Cadiedinia Fortunata Pia, who lived for [...] years [...]'; and [...] IVGI PIENTISS H S E '[...] to a most dutiful spouse who lies here'. At Alwoodley in Headingley a Roman stone coffin was found in 1995 at Beckett's Park.

The Romans had invaded Britain in AD 43. In AD 51 Caratacus, veteran British chieftain and king of the Catuvellauni, led his tribe along with the Silures and Ordovices against Publius Ostorius Scapula, the Roman governor. Scapula finally defeated Caratacus, capturing Caratacus's wife and daughter and taking his brothers prisoner. Caratacus himself fled to the Brigantes seeking asylum but, unfortunately for Caratacus, the queen of the Brigantes, Cartimandua (r. ca AD 43–ca AD 69), a Roman vassal, had him bound in chains and handed over to the Romans. Caratacus's reputation as a warrior preceded him and he was a star feature in Emperor Claudius's triumph in Rome marking his successful invasion. Cartimandua was amply rewarded. She divorced her husband Venutius for his armour-bearer Vellocatus; in AD 57 Venutius declared war against her and against the Romans, launching an unsuccessful invasion of Brigantia. However, in AD 69 Cartimandua had to be evacuated by the Romans after another attack by Venutius; their faithful client was no more, so, to control the troublesome Brigantes, the general Quintus Petillius Cerialis led the 9th Legion north from Lindum (Lincoln) across the Humber. Eboracum (York) was founded in AD 71 when Cerialis built a military fortress at the confluence of the rivers Ouse and Foss, some twenty-five miles from what was to become Leeds.

There is evidence too of Roman activity in Tadcaster and Wetherby. Tadaster (fifteen miles north-east from Leeds) was founded by the Romans who called it Calcaria, place of the lime burners, from the Latin word for lime, which, along with the Calcaria pub in Westgate, attests to the limestone deposits that have been quarried there for centuries. There was a Roman villa at nearby Kirkby Wharfe from which a tessellated pavement was excavated in 1711. Near Wetherby (thirteen miles north-east) is Dalton Parlours Roman villa, the only known example of its type in West Yorkshire. It comprises a main residential building, two bath blocks, other domestic buildings and outhouses and wells.

When the Romans left, the people of the area around Leeds resorted to local squabbling and intermittent fighting with outsiders. The Kingdom of Emlet was overrun by Edwin the Anglo-Saxon king of Northumbria in 617. However, Edwin's Christian church

The she-wolf (*lupa*) and Romulus and Remus – symbols of Rome and of Romanization. The mosaic, from the 4th century AD, was found at Aldborough and is now in the Leeds City Museum.

and palace were torched when the town was sacked by King Penda of Mercia after Edwin was killed at the battle of Hatfield Chase near Doncaster in 633.

In AD 655 the battle of the Winwaed took place at what is now Whinmoor on the outskirts of modern Leeds, near the river now known as Cock Beck in the Elmet, which runs through Penda's Fields in Leeds, before joining the River Wharfe. Here Penda was killed and decapitated by Edwin's nephew, the Christian King Oswiu of Bernicia (one of the two kingdoms of Northumbria), fighting to regain control of Northumbria. Christianity was established as the principal religion in Anglo-Saxon England after the Winwaed.

The first record of the name 'Leeds' comes from Bede in his *Historia Ecclesiastica* (Book II Chapter 14) around AD 731 when he mentions an altar from a church built by Edwin of Northumbria, in 'the region known as Loidis'. We learn from an 11th-century manuscript that in the 10th century, Loidis lay on the boundary between the Viking kingdom of Jorvik and the Welsh-speaking Kingdom of Strathclyde – Lancashire, Cumbria and south-western Scotland. The names Pen-y-Ghent, Craven, Hatfield, Aldborough and Stanwick provide more evidence of the Welsh influence. The name crops up again in the 1086 *Domesday Book* describing a settlement, in Old English, as *Ledes*. *Domesday* tells us that 'Ledes' has 'a priest, a church, a mill and 10 acres of meadow, 27 labourers, 4 freemen, 4 cottagers'. In 1086 Leeds had a population of some 200 people.

Military significance comes from *The Annals of Yorkshire,* 1862, from which we learn that 'In excavating for the foundations of the warehouses on the south side of West Bar, in 1836, the workmen discovered the remains of the Castle Moat. It appeared to have had a semicircular form, and to have terminated in the Mill Goite, extending considerably on each side of Scarbrough's Hotel, on which site the castle is supposed to have stood. A tower also stood near Lydgate in Woodhouse Lane, called Tower Hill; which was probably connected with the castle; but not a vestige of either fabric remains'.

After the Norman conquest Leeds itself was spared the devastation and depredation that was the fate of many settlements during the vengeful Harrying of the North by William I; however, Seacroft, Garforth, Coldcotes, Manston, Bramley, Beeston, Halton, and Allerton were comprehensively laid waste as vivid examples of how not to behave under the Normans.

We know from *The Leeds Guide* of 1837 that Ilbert de Lacy built a second castle around 1080 on Mill Hill – today's City Square – besieged by Stephen on his way to Scotland in 1139. The Castle of Leeds occupied the site surrounded in 1862 by Mill Hill, Bishopgate and the western part of Boar Lane. It was probably encircled by a moat, and an extensive park, as evidenced by the names Park Row and Park Square. According to the *Hardynge Chronicle* in 1399, Richard II was imprisoned at Leeds before being moved to Pontefract, where he was executed.

2. MILITARY LEEDS IN THE MIDDLE AGES

In the Later Middle Ages, Leeds remained without military significance; Pontefract was strategically more important. The Poll Tax of 1379 reveals that the population was less than 300 then, making Leeds one of the smaller towns in Yorkshire; Snaith, Ripon, Tickhill and Selby were all larger.

The Black Prince getting himself together in City Square. (Courtesy of Leodis © Leeds Library & Information Services)

The Black Prince

Edward of Woodstock KG (1330–76), better known as the Black Prince, was the eldest son of Edward III and Philippa of Hainault, and the father of Richard II of England. The equestrian statue in City Square took seven years to complete. It was cast in Belgium because it was too big for any British foundry; the Black Prince was brought to City Square by barge from Hull along the Aire & Calder Navigation and unveiled on 16 September 1903. The Black Prince has nothing to do with Leeds; he was a gift from Colonel Thomas Walter Harding, Lord Mayor of Leeds between 1898–9 and was just a historical figure Harding happened to admire, symbolizing as he did democracy and chivalry. The less said about his penchant for the *chevauchée* strategy (burning and pillaging towns and farms) the better.

Agriculture was still the principal economy. It was the Tudors who saw Leeds become an established cloth-trading town. The only real military activity was distinctly passive when Robert the Bruce's Scots army occupied Morley after the battle of Bannockburn in 1314, to add further misery to that caused by the failed harvest that year. The Scots were marching through the north of England burning, raping and pillaging as they went and exacting payments for truces. In 1323 a division of Scots troops wintered in Morley and left the place in ruins, destroying, among other places, St Mary's Chapel. It was reported that 'the residence of those barbarians for a whole winter at Morley, in the years 1322–23, was the greatest curse that the district ever knew'.

The Wars of the Roses

Leeds itself was little affected by the Wars of the Roses (1455–87) although there was plenty of action ten miles or so south and east which will have impinged on the growing town in terms of recruitment and certainly casualties which were nothing short of horrific.

The battle of Wakefield at Sandal Magna (ten miles south of Leeds) on 30 December 1460 saw forces loyal to Henry VI of the House of Lancaster, his queen, Margaret of Anjou, and their seven-year-old son Edward, Prince of Wales, drawn up against the army of Richard, Duke of York, the rival claimant to the throne. Ill-advisedly, Richard sortied from Sandal Castle and was killed in the ensuing battle along with the flower of the House of York; others, together with their family members were captured and executed. In the florid words of Edward Hall, Richard 'when he was in the plain ground between his castle and the town of Wakefield, he was environed on every side, like a fish in a net, or a deer in a buckstall; so that he manfully fighting was within half an hour slain and dead, and his whole army discomfited.'

As often, casualty figures are disputed: the near-contemporary *Gregory's Chronicle* gives 2,500 Yorkists and 200 Lancastrians killed, but other sources vary from 2,200 to only 700 Yorkists dead. Whatever, it was a decisive victory for the Lancastrians. Richard's titles, including his claim to the throne, passed to his eldest son Edward.

The next year saw the bloodiest battle of the war take place at Towton (sixteen miles south east of Leeds near Tadcaster) on 29 March 1461 with the Yorkists and Lancastrians squaring up between the villages of Towton and Saxton. This remains the biggest battle ever fought in England with between 50,000 and 80,000 soldiers in action including twenty-eight lords – almost half the country's peerage. It was also the bloodiest battle ever fought in England with up to 28,000 casualties: roughly a huge one per cent of the population of England at the time. More men probably died in the aftermath than in the battle itself because neither side gave quarter and nearby bridges collapsed under the weight of the armed men. The worst slaughter was at Bloody Meadow, where fugitives are said to have crossed the River Cock using the bodies of the fallen as a bridge.

This time, it was a decisive victory for the Yorkists. The Yorkist Edward, Duke of York, became King Edward IV (1461–83) having displaced the Lancastrian Henry VI (1422–61) as king.

The carnage that was the battle of Towton, by Paul Bishop.

Towton Battlefield Society re-enacting the battle of Towton. (Courtesy of the Towton Battlefield Society)

Hand-to-hand combat in the Wars of the Roses. (Photo Paul Kitchener)

3. LEEDS IN THE ENGLISH CIVIL WARS

It was only with the English Civil Wars, starting in 1642, that Leeds took centre stage and played a prominent role in things military. Indeed, Leeds was something of a swing-door town with Royalists replacing Roundheads and vice-versa at any opportunity. At the time, Leeds was still a small town but the seeds had been sown by the time of the Civil Wars to see it grow into one of England's great textile centres. Leeds, then, was largely a mercantile town with most merchants siding with the King against Parliament; was it not the King who had granted Leeds its lucrative Charter? The population exploded from 10,000 at the end of the 17th century to 30,000 by the end of the next. In the 1770s Leeds merchants went on to contribute almost a third of the country's woollen exports, valued at £1,500,000; seventy years previously the whole of Yorkshire accounted for only a fifth of the nation's exports.

After the inconclusive opening shots at Edgehill and Turnham Green in 1642, Charles I moved north to regain Yorkshire: Leeds, Bradford and Halifax were initially fertile recruiting and funding grounds for the Parliamentarians. In December 1642, Sir William Cavendish, the Earl of Newcastle, pushed Sir Thomas Fairfax and his father, Lord Ferdinando Fairfax, leaders of the Yorkshire Roundheads, from Tadcaster to Selby; at 11 a.m. on Tuesday 7 December 1642 the battle of Tadcaster took place around Tadcaster bridge between Fairfax's 900 men and the Earl of Newcastle's 8,000-strong Royalist army. The Royalists took the town.

Leeds soon became embroiled: Fairfax had found, paradoxically perhaps, 'the commonality of the town wholly at his command'. The town's involvement was nothing if not reluctant, reflecting as it did the feeling around the county as a whole: the gentry of both persuasions had tried in September to obviate hostilities by signing a treaty of neutrality vouching to disband all troops, to raise no more, to repel marauders of both sides, and to keep the peace. That all changed in mid-October 1642 when the Royalists, with a base in York and an eye on Bradford, dispatched 500 foot and 240 cavalry to Leeds with two cannon under Sir Thomas Glemham, Sir William Savile and others. The assault on Bradford failed. In December, Savile tried again at Bradford but was repulsed in a frenzy of clubs and scythes and retreated back to Leeds.

By early 1643 Leeds and Wakefield were garrisoned for the king under Sir William Savile with a paltry force of 500 cavalry and 1,500 foot. Savile ardently made preparations to defend the town, excavating a six-foot trench from St. John's Church north of what was Upper Headrow, down to Boar Lane and Swinegate to the banks of the Aire; building breastworks (temporary breast-height parapets) at the northern end of the bridge, and deploying demi-culverin cannon to cover Briggate. Leeds Bridge was barricaded off and fortified with cannon.

So began the **battle of Leeds**. Monday, 23 January saw Parliamentarian Sir Thomas Fairfax advance on Leeds with 3,000 horse and foot, 1,400 dragoons with men from Bradford, Halifax and the surrounding area adding up to nine troops of cavalry and dragoons, 1,000 musketeers and 2,000 clubmen (local militia, recruited to defend their locality). Savile had destroyed the bridge at Kirkstall so Fairfax was forced to cross the Aire at Apperley Bridge, whence he advanced on to Woodhouse Moor, calling for Savile to surrender, in writing, through a trumpeter sent out as a herald, 'for the use of King and Parliament'. Captain Mildmay occupied Hunslet Moor for the Roundheads.

Savile delivered the predictable 'disdainful reply', that 'he did not give answer to such frivolous tickets'. This was met by Fairfax with an attack around 2 p.m. in the middle of a snowstorm. The fighting soon enveloped the whole town; five companies of Parliamentarians took St John's Church, led by Fairfax and Sir Thomas Norcliffe, while a Scots Sergeant-Major Forbes attacked the breastworks near Boar Lane. A detachment of dragoons under Captain Mildmay, thirty musketeers and a thousand clubmen attacked Leeds Bridge from the south. At the head of one of the attacking groups was Jonathan

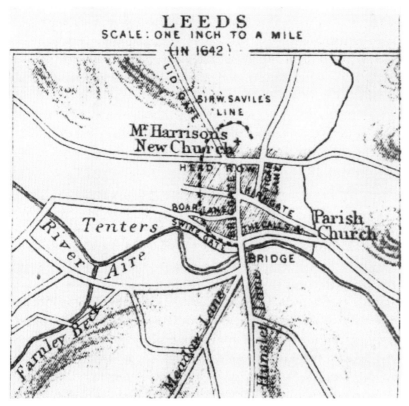

Leeds in 1642.

Schofield, the curate of Croston chapel in Halifax, who advanced carrying a bible in his hand and reciting the first verse of Psalm 6: 'God arises and then His enemies shall be scattered.' Fairfax later reported that the Royalist cannoneers were soon killed and 'bullets flew about our men's ears as thick as hail'.

By four o'clock the Parliamentarians were in Briggate and Boar Lane, while Savile, his troops and the curate took flight down Kirkgate back to their defences whence they swam their horses across the river; several men were drowned. The Parliamentarians took 600 prisoners, four colours, two brass cannon and arms and ammunition. In all about forty men were killed including twelve Parliamentarians. Fairfax took around 500 prisoners, all of whom he re immediately released on oath they did not take up arms against the Parliament again. Fairfax lost only twenty dead, another great victory for his 'well affected clubmen'.

The surviving Royalists fled to Wakefield which they quickly abandoned and retreated to York while Ferdinando Lord Fairfax recaptured Wakefield for the Parliamentarians. At the same time the Fairfaxes went on a recruitment and fund-raising campaign and raised £4,000 in Leeds alone.

Bouyed up by a much needed consignment of arms and ammunition delivered to York by Queen Henrietta Maria via Bridlington, the Royalists forced Fairfax to consolidate his forces in Leeds who created a diversion by having his son, Sir Thomas Fairfax, skirmish around Sherburn and Tadcaster.

The battle of Seacroft Moor on the moors of Whinmoor and Bramham east of Leeds followed next on 30 March 1643. Sir Thomas Fairfax advanced on Tadcaster via Sherburn to capture Tadcaster and destroy the bridge over the Wharfe. The aim was to mislead the Earl of Newcastle while he marched with his slow-moving artillery train back to Leeds into believing that he threatened the royalist city of York. Tadcaster was defended by only three or four hundred Royalist men, who took no time in fleeing York-ward. Fairfax destroyed the town's defences. (See map on page 1 of colour plates.)

But Newcastle reacted with a plan to intercept the numerically inferior Parliamentarians. He delegated his lieutenant-general, Lord George Goring, to carry this out with twenty troops of horse, 2,000 men, seven times Fairfax's cavalry numbers. Heavily outnumbered, Fairfax ordered his infantry back to Leeds across Bramham Moor while he stayed behind with the cavalry to hold up Goring's advance. Fairfax's ramshackle force was made up mainly of musketeers, clubmen and only three troops of regular cavalry. Although strong in musketeers, these were of little advantage on the open moorland, vulnerable as they were to cavalry attack with few, if any, pikemen to protect the musketeers and clubmen. Meanwhile, Fairfax senior led the remaining 1,500 men, ordnance and ammunition back to Leeds.

Predictably, Fairfax was heavily defeated and took many casualties, although he himself escaped with a few cavalrymen back to Leeds. His troops had made matters worse by

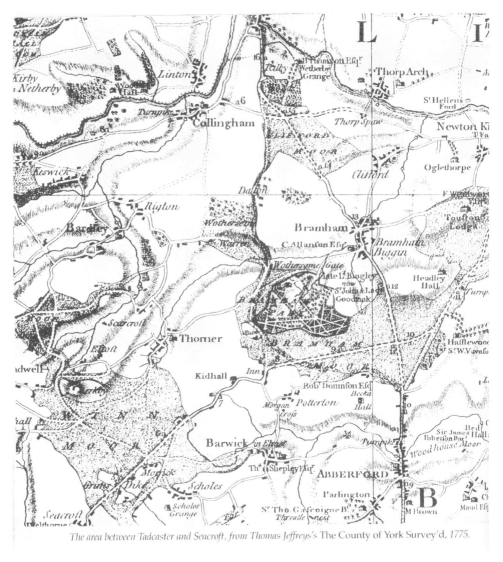

The area between Tadcaster and Seacroft, from Thomas Jeffreys's The County of York Survey'd, *1775.*

The area between Tadcaster and Seacroft.

pausing to refresh themselves; had Goring pressed home his attack immediately, then the war in Yorkshire might have ended on Seacroft Moor, properly Whinmoor.

The nearby Cock Beck, which ran through the battlefield, reputedly ran red with blood for several days after. The Parliamentarians had lost over 1,000 infantry: only a handful of their cavalry got back alive to the main Parliament army in Leeds. Acting as a kind of war correspondent, Cavendish's wife, the Duchess of Newcastle, reported that over 800 prisoners were taken by the Royalists. It has been estimated that Fairfax lost 200 men killed

The battle of Seacroft Moor, 30 March 1643.

and about a thousand taken prisoner. He tells us in his memoirs that 'we were so busied about releasing the prisoners that were taken at Seacroft most of them being countrymen [local clubmen], whose wives and children were still importunate for their release, which was as earnestly endeavoured by us, but no conditions were accepted: so as their continual cries, tears, and importunities, compelled us to think of some way to redeem these men; and we thought of attempting Wakefield'.

This explains the audacious Parliamentarian assault on Wakefield, in May 1643, where the prisoners were held when, with 1,100 men, Fairfax attacked Wakefield which was garrisoned by about 3,000 men plus cavalry.

The **battle of Wakefield**: Sir Thomas Fairfax tells us that the royalist force comprised around 900 or so troops with four guns. A more plausible motive for the attack on Wakefield though, was that the Earl of Newcastle had moved his arsenal there, a fact which Fairfax knew through his spies. The Royalist ammunition was a desirable prize. He may also have had an eye on the bustling food markets of Wakefield which provisioned the 'well-affected' people of Leeds, Bradford and Halifax. The Parliamentarians, however, got their numbers very wrong, seriously underestimating the strength of the Royalist garrison. The 900 or so troops they had assumed were actually 3,000 infantry and seven troops of cavalry. By the time the Royalist troops in Wakefield became aware of the advance of a strong Parliamentary force 'most of the officers and the governor

[Sir Francis Mackworth] were enjoying a convivial all-night bowls party at Heath House on the far side of the River Calder', half an hour or so away and not taking into account that most of the officers were inebriated. Inevitably, the Parliamentary cavalry drove the Royalist troops out of Wakefield. Fairfax won the day, calling it 'more a miracle than a victory'. (See map on page 2 of colour plates.)

Those men captured at Seacroft were released and, as a bonus, General Goring (who went to the Tower) and 1,400 others were taken prisoner. The full toll reads as follows: the Parliamentary troops captured from the Royalists twenty-seven colours of foot, three standards of horse, General Goring, three lieutenant-colonels (including Sir Thomas Bland, lieutenant-colonel to Sir George Wentworth's regiment), one major, eleven captains, five lieutenants, fifteen ensigns and around 1,500 soldiers. One major and one captain who were wounded were left in Wakefield as prisoners. In addition, four royalist cannon and the immense ammunition reserve of the Earl of Newcastle were captured along with £6,000 in cash. A costly night for the king all round. The Roundheads lost seven men.

The battle of Adwalton Moor (seven miles south west of Leeds) was fought on 30 June 1643, the Royalists under the Earl of Newcastle with some 4,000 foot and 3,000 horse and dragoons; he was advancing on Parliamentarian-held Bradford with 10,000 men against Fairfax, the Parliamentary commander who had 4,000 foot and 1,500 horse and dragoons supported by 'clubmen', most of whom were armed with agricultural implements.

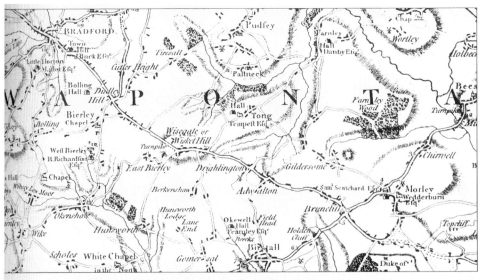

The area around Adwalton Moor, from Thomas Jeffreys's The County of York Survey'd, *1775.*

The area around Adwalton Moor.

The Royalist army also had the advantage of a powerful artillery battery including two two-and-a-half-ton demi-cannon nicknamed 'Gog' and 'Magog' with their thirty-five-pound shells. The Royalists, though, had been weakened at the battle of Wakefield through the loss of many foot soldiers, an area in which were under strength anyway, the capture of the Earl of Newcastle's arsenal and the capture of his cavalry commander, General George Goring.

Newcastle temporarily abandoned his assault on Bradford and retreated to York before resuming his Bradford attack in mid-June 1643. Howley Hall, a mansion near Morley fortified with 140 men of Sir John Savile's regiment owned by Savile was attacked first, looted and taken on 22 June; Newcastle then continued towards Bradford with 12,000 men. (See map on page 3 of colour plates.)

Seeking to avoid a siege, Fairfax came out to meet the Royalist army at Adwalton but lost the battle; the attack by Royalist pikemen was made by the Earl of Newcastle's own regiment led by Lieutenant-Colonel Posthumous Kirton of the Dutch service. Sir Thomas Fairfax in his report says that the attack was carried out by 'one Colonel Skirton, a wild and desperate man'.

The Earl of Newcastle reached Bradford the same night as the battle and bombarded the town the next day. Soon, the Parliamentary garrison tried to break out; Sir Thomas

The battle of Adwalton Moor, 30 June 1643, by Jean Meulener.

Fairfax and General Gifford left the town with fifty horse while the rest of the garrison surrendered. They lost 500 men with a further 1,400 taken prisoner at Adwalton with 300 more surrendering in Bradford.

Sir Thomas Fairfax further tells us that four Parliamentary troopers stripped and pillaged the body of a Royalist commander, Colonel George Heron, who had been killed in the second charge on the Parliamentary right wing. Soon after, Sir Thomas saw a Royalist cannon ball hit and kill two of the four troopers, badly injuring the other two. Sir Thomas recorded that it was 'a remarkable passage of Divine Retribution' for their reprehensible conduct and a salutary warning to other potential 'villains' or body looters.

The Royalists thereby strengthened their control of Yorkshire; at the same time it was nothing short of a disaster for the Parliamentarians. After Marston Moor, Adwalton Moor is considered to be the second-most important Civil War action fought in the north. It was due to Adwalton Moor that Scots armies were invited to join the war on the side of the Parliamentarians. Leeds was the next to fall to the Royalists when 700 prisoners broke out, captured the arsenal and held on until Newcastle arrived. Fairfax retreated to Selby and the Humber with a handful of men. From Barton-on-Humber he crossed the river to Hull, his army or what was left of it in total disarray.

The battle of Marston Moor (twenty-four miles north-east of Leeds) was, of course, the defining battle of the Civil War in the north. It was fought on 2 July 1644 with the forces of Lord Fairfax, the Earl of Manchester and the Scottish Covenanters under the Earl of Leven who defeated the Royalists led by Prince Rupert of the Rhine and the Earl of Newcastle. The north of England was now lost to Charles I.

On 9 February 1646 Charles I came to Leeds as prisoner when, after his surrender to the Scottish Presbyterian army at Kelham, near Newark, he was taken to Newcastle and, after nine months of negotiations, was handed over to the Parliamentarians for £1,000. Then he was transported to Leeds where he spent a night in the Red Hall, in Upper Head Row. Things were to get much worse for the king.

On Cossins's map of 1725 Red Hall is the large house at the junction of the Upper Head Row with Lands Lane. Built in 1628, it was the first house in Leeds to be built of brick, hence the name. The gardens at the rear extended to where Albion Place is today. Charles was confined in a room at Red Hall, afterwards known as the King's Chamber; his stay in Leeds is also attested by local names King Charles's Street and King Charles's Croft. On the other hand, Cromwell is remembered in the city of Leeds with Cromwell Street and Cromwell Heights off Cromwell Street: three high-rise tower blocks in Burmantofts.

The West Yorkshire Regiment

Our first record of the West Yorkshire Regiment is as 'Hales Regiment of Foot' in 1685 when it supported the 1st Duke of Monmouth in the attempt to overthrow James II; the battle of Sedgemoor brought an end to that. The regiment then saw action serving William III during the Nine Years' War fighting at the siege of Namur (1695) and then in Scotland during the first Jacobite Rebellion. The regiment garrisoned Gibraltar for fifteen years and was present at the Great Siege of Gibraltar in 1727 during the Anglo-Spanish War. The regiment returned to Scotland during the second Jacobite Rebellion and fought at the battles of Falkirk and Culloden.

In 1751 the West Yorkshires became the 14th Regiment of Foot with a further eight years' service in Gibraltar. In 1766 it was posted to Nova Scotia and Boston, moving to the West Indies for three years from 1772. The 14th returned to America during the American War of Independence (1775–83) fighting at the battle of Great Bridge (1775); however, in 1776 the regiment was disbanded while the officers returned to England to recruit. The regiment was resuscitated in 1782 as the 14th (Bedfordshire) Regiment of Foot.

In 1881 as a result of the Childers Reforms the regiment, by then 14th (Buckinghamshire – The Prince of Wales's Own) Regiment of Foot, was retitled as The Prince of Wales's Own (West Yorkshire Regiment) and went on to see service in the Gold Coast (now Ghana) in 1895, the Boer War (1899–1902) and both world wars. In 1959 the regiment was merged with the East Yorkshire Regiment to form the Prince of Wales's Own Regiment of Yorkshire. In 2006 there was yet more change when the West Yorkshire Regiment was amalgamated with The Green Howards and The Duke of Wellington's Regiment to form The Yorkshire Regiment.

4. LEEDS AND THE JACOBITE RISINGS; CHARTISTS

The first rebellion was in 1715 when the exiled Catholic Charles Edward Stuart, 'The Young Pretender' or Bonnie Prince Charlie made an attempt to win back the throne for the house of Stuart from the reigning house of Hanover. No Jacobite army ever set foot in Leeds in 1715 or 1745 but the threat to the crown resonated in the city. Indeed, the Brotherton Library at the University of Leeds has several important Jacobite documents, including an inventory of James II's goods (drawn up in 1703), a grant of a marriage portion from James to Princess Louisa (1698) and a copy of James II's will.

At the time it is the so-called 'Leeds Riot' for which the city is most remembered – a manifestation of the anxieties felt by some of the Whigs of Leeds fearing the monarchy to be under threat from a French invasion. The Tory mayor, Solomon Pollard, was rumoured to have described his taking of the oath of loyalty to George I as 'the bitterest pill'. Furthermore, the Leeds parish bell-ringers had unaccountably delayed their usual Thursday night practice until Friday – which happened to be the birthday of the Young Pretender. To make matters worse, the practice session went on some three hours longer than usual.

Three officers of the local dragoons read this as the catalyst for an uprising and marched their soldiers through the town late that night to the beat of a drum. It all fizzled out, despite the crowds that had gathered out of curiosity. The highly spun report that Secretary of State Stanhope in London received was that Leeds had celebrated the Pretender's birthday with 'the ringing of Bells, Bonfires, & all other marks of Publick Joy, that there was a great meeting of Magistrates, clergy, etc ... who drank his health & that if the soldiery had not awed the Mob, the issue wou'd have been of ye worst Consequence'. Pollard and others were summoned to London to explain themselves. Alderman William Cookson penned a frantic letter to Ralph Thoresby and was arrested as a result, suspected of colluding with the Jacobites. The charges were later dropped.

The second Jacobean rising began on 23 July 1745 when The Young Pretender left Nantes with seven supporters (including one Englishman and three Irishmen) and landed near Mallaig in the Western Isles. He led 3,000 men under arms in Scotland, mostly raw recruits, while the best part of the British army was in Flanders fighting the French. Nevertheless, Stuart gained the support of 1,000 Camerons and raised the royal standard at Glenfinnan on 19 August; he captured Perth and then, on 17 September, Edinburgh. On the 21st Stuart defeated an army under Sir John Cope at Prestonpans; he stayed in Edinburgh to prepare his army and on 31 October, he set off south to march on London via Newcastle, York and Leeds and Derby.

Among others, Henry Ingram of Temple Newsam was appalled – he had just decorated his Long Hall with heads of the King and of his family. Henry Ibbetson of Red Hall offered to raise, at his own expense, 100 men to support the regular companies and defend the king and 'the Illustrious House of Hanover'. He later received a baronetcy. Houses were raided and searched, the horses of Catholics were appropriated and anonymous, incriminating notes were investigated. General Wade, meanwhile, passed through the area en route to Newcastle where he was outmaneuvered by the Scots; it was John Wesley who brought the bad news to Leeds on 5 November, Bonfire Night. Wesley found a town 'full of bonfires, and people shouting, firing of guns, cursing and swearing, as the English manner of keeping holidays is'. His sobering news cleared the streets immediately.

By 22 November the relentless progress south of the Scots led to the formation of the Leeds Parliament, Leeds being the natural place to consolidate a defence against the rebel armies. Panic was growing, valuable trade with Lancashire was disrupted and in early December a band of citizens proposed arming themselves to face the rebels. They were dissuaded by the rational argument that they would be slaughtered to a man and Leeds would suffer heavy reprisals. Although the Jacobites bypassed the city on the way to Derby, General Wade occupied Leeds, camping on Woodhouse Moor.

Culloden extinguished the threat once and for all but it was concluded locally that Leeds had come close to a sacking by the Scots and the vulnerability of the town should be reduced by stationing troops nearby. We learn from Ensign Storr's orderly book entry for 11 May 1761 that this indeed happened. However, the battalion in question was obviously not a crack fighting force for he notes that on a route march the following day to Knaresbrough, 'Any Soldier who appears Drunk … will be March'd prisoner, Tryd by a Court Martial and severly punished.'

Chartists

Nearly a century later, Leeds was at the centre of the Chartist movement – the demand for the franchise to be extended to working-class men after the 1832 Reform Act. Feargus O'Connor, one of the leading Chartists, published *The Northern Star*, a chartist propaganda sheet, in Leeds. During the General Strike of 1842 Leeds's activism manifested itself in the Plug Riots when crowds of workers went from factory to factory pushing in the boiler plugs to wreck the boilers and bring production to a halt. Leeds council was desperate, writing to the government in London that never before had Leeds experienced 'distress so universal, so prolonged, so exhaustive and so ruinous'. The local special constables were equipped with 30,000 staves, specially made, curfews were imposed and pubs closed early. Hunslet, Holbeck and the west of the town saw rioting on 17 August; 1,600 extra special constables were sworn in and deployed to help the regulars. The 17th Lancers under Prince George of Cambridge and the Yorkshire Regiment under Lieutenant-Colonel William Beckett were mobilized in the town.

Mills at Farnley, Wortley and Pudsey had been 'plugged' and Armley was next. To meet the threat a huge force of police and military was deployed. First were the regular police with cutlasses and heavy batons, followed by 1,200 special constables three or four abreast with their staves. The army units brought up the rear: a troop of the 17th Lancers, eighteen men of the 187th Infantry (Yorkshire Regiment) bayonets fixed, a battery from the Royal Horse Artillery with gun and the Ripon Troop of Yeomanry. Meanwhile the mob had decommissioned Temple Mill in Holbeck. They were met by the Lancers and their weaponry; the Riot Act was read and the mob dispersed – only to reform at the Maclea and Marsh Mill in Dewsbury Road. Back-up from the military was requested but the specials made thirty-eight arrests before the army arrived. The police read the Riot Act again and the mob finally dispersed. Sentences included ten years' transportation.

Greenwood & Batley

During the Crimean War (1853–6) the engineering firm of Greenwood & Batley won the contract to make machines for weapons manufacture for the arsenals at Woolwich and the Royal Small Arms Factory, Enfield. At the end of the war the company also participated, fittingly enough, in staging the illuminations in Leeds to celebrate the victory. Fairburn Greenwood & Batley provided 'a brilliant device in gas consisting of lines of gas along the architecture of the Grecian façade and enclosing two large stars and, V and N in large Roman capitals'.

In August 1856 the great and the good of Leeds entertained Lord Cardigan, leader of the Charge of the Light Brigade in the Crimean War, in the banqueting hall of the Stock Exchange in Leeds. The 'People of Yorkshire' presented him with a sword costing £250.

Nineteenth-century foreign politics were never a strong point at Greenwood & Batley. 'Arms and the (wrong) man' might have been an appropriate company motto. During the American Civil War (1861–5) Greenwood & Batley were happily supplying arms to the Confederates: 'It appears that in this case certain goods were manufactured by the plaintiffs, Thos. Greenwood and John Batley, carrying on business under the name or style of Greenwood and Batley, of Leeds for the Confederate States of America, at a time when they were recognized by this country as belligerents.'

In February 1878 they faced 'an action brought by General Berdan of the United States, America, to recover from the defendants, who are engineers and machinists, carrying on business and having manufactories at Leeds, a sum of £5,500 odd, by way of commission on orders relating to the manufacture of guns for the Russian Government'. Russia and the USA were not at war at the time, however Hiram Berdan claimed that Greenwood & Batley had supplied machines to produce his 'Berdan Rifle' in the Russian Tula Factory and that he was therefore owed commission. The Berdan Rifle became standard issue to the Russian army from 1869–91.

5. LEEDS VOLUNTEERS AND RIFLES; LUDDITES

The original regiment of volunteers was raised in 1782 only to be disbanded five years later. The French Revolution forced a change of mind on the volunteer issue in 1794 when very real fears of a French invasion of England and possible insurrection by the English working classes were at their height. Militarily, England was very weak; to offset this volunteer numbers nationally rose to more than 380,000 men. The ruling Tory corporation and magistrates in Leeds were fully supportive of a band of loyal townsmen in arms to quell any lower order insurrection.

By April of 1794, 200 'gentlemen' had signed up to the Leeds Volunteers, commanded by the experienced Thomas Lloyd. The colours were presented on Chapeltown Moor to the accompaniment of a three-volley gun salute and manoeuvres. Military activity was interspersed with dinners, concerts and theatre performances laid on by a grateful corporation. A crowd of 60,000 came to watch a review of the volunteers from Leeds, Halifax, Bradford, Huddersfield and Wakefield on the Moor in May 1795. The Volunteers acted as a fire brigade: one of their biggest shouts was a fire at Marshall & Benyon's Mill which was aflame for three days, killing eight and injuring more than thirty.

An attempt to set up a Leeds volunteer cavalry squadron failed, but in 1797 Napoleon's victory in northern Italy over the Austrian–Russian coalition left an anxious England feeling yet more vulnerable; the cavalry project was revived and a riding school for gentlemen and ladies was established under the equestrian tuition of a Sergeant Lamb on Tuesdays, Wednesdays and Saturdays while the other days saw the Volunteer Cavalry put through their paces. It was then realized that in the event of the volunteer infantry and cavalry being mobilized, Leeds would be left undefended. Accordingly, an armed association, a militia in effect, was established under Thomas Butler of Kirkstall Forge around 1798, supported by the firm of Benjamin Gott.

Luddites

In November 1799 Messrs Johnson of Beeston ignited what would become the Luddite issue in Leeds when they insisted on installing a gig mill (to replace the croppers). A mob of workers responded by burning down the mill. Fearing more trouble the magistrates had Colonel Lloyd deploy drummers throughout the night to summon the Volunteers quickly should the need arise. Things continued to get increasingly tense and by 1812 Luddism was much in evidence in the town. By now the volunteers had been replaced by the Leeds Local Militia who were considered inadequate for the crisis. So, to defend the town, the Scots Greys, Queen's Militia and the West Kent Militia were posted to Leeds. The *Leeds Mercury* reported that 'at night in particular, Leeds and Huddersfield have, with their picquets and military patrols, assumed more the appearance of Garrison Towns than of the peaceful abodes of trade and industry'.

The Treaty of Amiens in 1802 saw the infantry hand in their weapons; this proved to be somewhat presumptuous and premature because the following year hostilities with France resumed and the soldiers were promptly invited to re-enrol. This they did in spades, with 1,400 signing up to form two battalions under Lloyd. Training began but with no weapons; the rifles were on order from Prussia and only arrived in Leeds some weeks later. A short-lived threat of invasion by Napoleon who had assembled at Boulogne with a fleet of landing craft was met with an order for the Leeds volunteers to stand by 'with shirts, shoes and brushes all packed up all ready'.

In 1804 1,100 of the infantry agreed to be put on permanent stand-by with the War Office until they 'acquired the necessary proficiency in military discipline'; the two battalions then went to York for three weeks' training and then on to more training at Doncaster. 1806 saw severe economic hardship in Leeds with punitive measures by the French and the Americans blighting local trade; in 1808 the volunteers were replaced by the Leeds Local Militia whose main preoccupation now was not Napoleon, but domestic revolution. The battle of Waterloo in 1815, however, eased the situation immeasurably to the extent that the militia was disbanded.

The situation had not improved by 1819 with gig mills and shearing frames slashing the workforces; poverty in Leeds was still at critical levels. The government responded by reducing the employment of the croppers still further and by voting £24,000 for a new barracks at Buslingthorpe between the Roundhay and Chapel Allerton roads.

The story of the Leeds volunteers resumes in 1859 when the call for a local volunteer rifle corps went out, again in a response to possible French invasion. This was met with an enthusiastic response with famous Leeds families like the Kitsons (railway engineers and builders of Aerolite in 1851) and Luptons signing up. The new regiment, the Leeds Rifles, was quickly raised with financial support from the city's business leaders, not least Joshua Tetley of brewery fame from whom a number of the regiment's companies were recruited, as well as commanding officers and honorary colonels. The Leeds Rifles was officially adopted as the 11th Yorkshire West Riding Rifle Volunteer Corps (RVC); in May 1860 it subsumed the 22nd (Leeds) Yorkshire West Riding RVC, and the combined unit, now the size of a battalion, was renumbered the 7th West Riding RVC. It was initially headquartered next to Leeds Town Hall.

Tetley's was not the only fertile commercial recruiting ground. No. 3 Company was formed from the Woollen & Allied Trades; Kitson's at Monk Bridge Iron Works, Fairbairn's at Wellington Foundry and Greenwood & Batley at Armley all populated

An officer of the Leeds Rifles, from a watercolour by W. R. Younghusband.

regimental companies. Other companies were recruited by district: No. 4 was the East Ward Company and the Chapeltown Company was No. 5.

Money was always a problem for the RVCs: government funding was decidedly scarce so they fell back on members' subscriptions and the generosity of their officers. One such officer generous to the Leeds Rifles was Captain Thomas Kinnear, a partner in the textile firm Benjamin Gott & Son at Wellington Bridge and Armley Mills; he lent over £1,100 of his own money to pay off the unit's debts.

The main role of the RVCs was home defence, but members often volunteered for service overseas in other units. For example, three or more members of the Leeds Rifles served in the British Legion and fought with Garibaldi in his 1860 campaign in Naples.

The Childers Reforms of 1881 saw the Leeds Rifles attached to its local county regiment, the Prince of Wales's Own (West Yorkshire Regiment) as the regiment's 3rd Volunteer Battalion in 1887. The Leeds Rifles were allowed to retain their rifle-green uniforms even though the West Yorkshires were a red-coated regiment.

The Rifles then purchased Carlton Barracks, at Carlton Hill in Leeds, and converted it to its regimental HQ. The barracks were situated on Barrack Road, built on an eleven-acre site by Craven & Co. in 1820 at a cost of £28,000. The barracks included soldiers' quarters, officers' accommodation, canteen, stables, hospital and a riding school. In 1897, the barracks were also occupied by the 21st Lancers. Between 1909 and 1916 the Leeds Rifles used part of the engine shed at Neville Hill as a drill hall. The Leeds Rifles met at the old riding school and parade ground for eighty years, until they moved to Harewood Barracks in 1967. The barracks were demolished in 1988.

In 1908 the Volunteer Force became the Territorial Force and the unit expanded to two battalions, each over 1,000 strong; they were known as the 7th and 8th (Leeds Rifles) battalions, The Prince of Wales's Own (West Yorkshire Regiment) (TA).

Around 1911 C Company's Scouting and Skirmishing Team were winners of the huge Bingham Trophy, made in Sheffield in 1893 and, at over three feet high and 11 feet in circumference, is the largest piece of sterling silver hollow ware ever made. It cost £800 and was to be awarded to the winning Yorkshire Volunteers battalion in the annual field-firing competition on the orders of Colonel J. E. Bingham.

Tetley's and the Leeds Volunteers

Horses were much in demand by the Royal Horse Artillery, the Yorkshire Hussars and the Army Service Corps; at least 500 were requisitioned including the shires of Joshua Tetley.

On 5 August 1914, the day after war was declared, Tetley's received a letter requisitioning eight shire horses, two covered wagons, two shaft wherries and four sets of artillery harness. The horses were seen to be invaluable logistics support: they could haul up to three times their own weight and constituted a priceless means of transporting artillery and supplies. At weights of up to just under one ton that was a considerable load; there is a record of a six-shire team pulling an eight-ton truck out of the Flanders mud in 1915. The enlisted horses were Arabi, Rover, Stanley, Spark, Bruce, Dolphin, Peter and Jim. If they survived the war, and millions of horses did not, they would have been left in the care of French and Belgian farmers. Sixty per cent did survive. Later that month, twelve more shires were conscripted and sent to France – Ball, Clare, Farmer, Harry, Briton, Lion, Peter, Tartar, Musket, Ponty, Tory and Royal – to serve with 1st West Riding Field Ambulance. The man who requisitioned them, Sergeant-Major H. Hayden of the Royal Army Service Corps, reported that four years and two months later, ten were alive and still working well. Briton had been wounded and Clare had suffered shell shock.

Leeds had a long reputation of providing manpower when the call came. As noted, from the time of the French Revolution, from 1789 until 1799 when the English feared an invasion by the French, Leeds men were always there. Our first record of a Tetley man joining up comes with a notice in the *Leeds Intelligencer* of 9 January 1797 announcing the formation of the Leeds Volunteer Cavalry at a meeting held at the Old King's Arms, Leeds, inviting interested parties to sign up. Twenty-five men enrolled, including William Tetley, father or brother of Joshua. Later, Isaac Rimington Tetley, Joshua's eldest brother, eschewed a career in the family brewing firm for service in the Leeds Volunteer Infantry (the predecessors of the Rifles) from 1803, and then, when this unit was disbanded in 1808, the Leeds Local Militia from 1808, reaching the rank of captain before the militia too was disbanded in 1814.

In 1860, a year after the Leeds Rifles were formed, No. 9 Company was the Joshua Tetley Company, Tetley's Own, and could count Captain Francis William Tetley in its ranks. Such was the enthusiasm in the brewery that the sixty-six recruits were all signed up on day one and sworn in on 31 October when the brewery closed for the purpose of recruiting. William Brocklesby, an apprentice cooper of Portland Crescent, Leeds, was the youngest at 13 – probably destined to be a bugle boy. Bugles were the instrument rifle regiments drilled to; drums were the instrument of choice for all the rest. John R. Foster was 14, a clerk from Eldon Place, Woodhouse; William Henry Mellish, a clerk from Westfield Cottage, Headingley was 15, as was Zaccheus Thornes a cellarman of Folly Lane, Beeston Hill. The average height for brewery recruits was 5 foot 7.8 inches and the average age was twenty-seven.

Over time, fifty-six per cent of the brewery work force joined the volunteers. Leaving the employ of Tetley for whatever reason meant immediate discharge from the Leeds Rifles. The drill sergeant at the 4th West York Militia at Carlton Barracks, Sergeant Neville, was engaged to drill the Rifles recruits. According to the scrupulously kept records of efficiency, No. 9 Company came out best in 1868. Marksmanship skills were honed at Leeds

Artillery range at Halton – transport and refreshments courtesy of Tetley's – where one colour sergeant, John Musgrave, head cellarman of Priestley Buildings, Dewsbury Road, was a regular cup winner.

Leeds Rifles in 1900 included Honorary Colonel Charles Ryder and Lieutenant Charles Harold Tetley; Ryder had been a stalwart of the unit since its formation, for example giving up annual leave from the brewery to train with a regular army regiment and pass on what he had learned.

Uniforms cost £3 8s 7d, half paid by Tetley's and half by the soldier to be repaid in weekly instalments of not less than 3d. Local military tailor, Thomas M'Intyre, made the uniforms. A clothing committee monitored his work and prices, the committee comprising head cellarmen, a clerk, a storeroom labourer, a yard foreman and a mash-room labourer.

Belts and pouches were paid for by the Leeds Volunteer Corps and rifles came courtesy of the government. There were, however, subscription fees which the brewery looked after. Terms of service were: 'Volunteers are likely to be called out for active service only in the case of actual invasion, appearance of enemy in force on coast of Great Britain, or rebellion or insurrection within the same.'

Training involved drill every evening from 6.15 to 7.30 after a twelve-hour shift; but a fifteen-minute break was permitted. Once a month in winter, No. 9 Company went on a seven-mile route march on the Saturday night nearest to the full moon. British industry generally has Tetley volunteers to thank for the five-and-a-half-day working week which the brewery introduced in April 1861, allowing their workers who were in the volunteers (half the workforce that is) time off on a Saturday afternoon to attend drill practice. Other companies followed suit.

The Fenian scare

In the event, the Tetley Volunteers were only ever called up once, during the Fenian scare in 1867. The Fenians were the Irish Republican Brotherhood, a nationalist organization which launched an unsuccessful revolt in Ireland in 1867 and carried out a number of actions against the British until they were eclipsed by the IRA in the early 20th century. One such anticipated action was a demonstration outside Leeds Town Hall on 15 December where the weapons of the Leeds Rifles, as noted, were secured in the bridewell there. The demonstration never materialized so the Rifles were able to retire without having fired a shot.

1st (Leeds) Yorkshire West Riding Artillery Volunteer Corps

Amid fears of an invasion in 1860 the Secretary at War proposed the formation of volunteer artillery corps to strengthen Britain's coastal defences. The 1st (Leeds) Yorkshire West Riding Artillery Volunteer Corps was one of the Yorkshire units, formed on 2 August 1860. Initially they fulfilled a role as coastal artillery with 32-pounder guns. By 1871, the 1st had expanded to eight batteries. From 1889 they were re-formed and classed as 'position artillery', armed with 40-pounder RBL guns (which used William Armstrong's new and innovative rifled breech-loading mechanism). In 1892 the corps were again re-organized as part of the Western Division Royal Artillery and were titled 1st, 2nd and 4th West Riding of Yorkshire Volunteer Artillery, with headquarters at Leeds, Bradford and Sheffield respectively. After 1902, they became the 1st, 2nd and 4th West Riding of Yorkshire Royal Garrison Artillery (Volunteers) and were re-equipped with 4.7-inch QF (quick-firing) guns drawn by steam tractors.

As a result of Haldane's Territorial and Reserve Forces Act 1907, volunteer units were merged to form the Territorial Force (subsequently, the Territorial Army in 1921); they enjoyed the same role as before, but with the addition of acting as back-up to the regular army if and when the need arose. As a result, the 1st (Leeds) Yorkshire West Riding Artillery Volunteer Corps became the 1st West Riding Brigade Royal Field Artillery (TF) with its HQ at Fenton Street.

2nd West Riding (Leeds) Engineer Volunteer Corps

The 2nd West Riding (Leeds) Engineer Volunteer Corps was formed on 21 May 1861. They started life as the 2nd West Yorkshire Royal Engineer Volunteers with 500 volunteers signed up in their first year. Their dashing uniforms comprised a scarlet coat, dark trousers with a scarlet stripe and a cap with a large, white hair plume. By 1865 they were an impressive 1,000 men strong and had premises opposite the Theatre Royal. In 1868 the unit moved into Gibraltar Barracks purchased for £5,538 in 1891. The barracks were in Claypit Lane at the junction with Grove House Lane, the base of the Royal Corps of Signals, 49th (West Yorkshire) Divisional Signals. Gibraltar Barracks was extended in 1889 when the entrance portcullis was built. The unit became the 49th (West Riding) Divisional Signal Company in 1920 when it re-formed. It saw active service in both world wars before disbanding in 1967.

Yorkshire Hussars Yeomanry (Alexandra, Princess of Wales's Own)

Northallerton was the venue of the first meeting held to discuss the raising of yeomanry units in Yorkshire, on 12 June 1794. It included nobility, gentry, clergy, freeholders and others. At a further meeting on 13 July it was agreed to form two regiments of West Riding yeomanry. The 1st, or Southern, Regiment became the

James Millington, one of Tetley's volunteers in No. 9 Company, the Leeds Rifles (Tetley's Own) which he joined in April 1861, age eighteen. He lived at 6 Mark Lane. (Courtesy of Colonel R. Addyman and originally published in Lackey's *Quality Pays*)

Yorkshire Dragoons, and the 2nd, or Northern, Regiment was the forerunner of the Yorkshire Hussars. The five troops of the 2nd or Northern Regiment of West Riding Yeomanry Cavalry were raised at Skipton, Knaresborough, Leeds, Wakefield and Tadcaster. The Hussars were particularly active in the Second Boer War, as outlined in the following chapter.

The uniform comprised scarlet jackets with green collars and cuffs, and light cavalry helmets. In March 1802 they were disbanded after the Peace of Amiens but in July three troops offered to renew their services and were accepted: the Knaresborough Troop under Captain Robert Harvey, Tadcaster Troop under Lord Hawke, and Aberford under Lieutenant Bainbridge. Four further troops were added in October. In September 1817 two more troops were raised, from Leeds, under Captain William Beckett.

On 11 January 1819, the regiment was converted to a hussar regiment as the Yorkshire Hussar Regiment of Yeomanry Cavalry and in 1864, to mark the Queen's Jubilee, the Yorkshire Hussars became Yorkshire Hussars (Alexandra, Princess of Wales's Own) or Yorkshire Hussars (APWO).

In 1842 on 3 June, the regiment was under arms until 31 August assisting the military in the outbreak of serious Chartist riots in the West Riding. They were on duty in the Leeds and Bradford area. One troop under Captain York had to charge the mob at Cleckheaton (eleven miles south-west of Leeds).

The Territorial Act of 1908 led to the Yorkshire Hussars, Yorkshire Dragoons and the East Riding Yeomanry being merged as the Yorkshire Mounted Brigade. A Squadron was raised at Leeds (with a drill station at Ilkley). In 1912 the brigade trained at Bulford on Salisbury Plain, the first time that the regiment had trained outside the county in peacetime.

6. LEEDS AND THE SECOND ANGLO-BOER WAR

Leeds Town Hall is home to The Leeds Boer War Memorial, a brass plaque that lists those who served (458 names) and those who died (13 names); it was unveiled in November 1902. The names are listed by regiment, by rank, by surname, and by decoration. The inscription reads: 'THIS TABLET WAS PLACED HERE BY ORDER OF THE CITY COUNCIL TO RECOGNISE AND TO COMMEMORATE THE PATRIOTISM OF THE VOLUNTEERS FROM THIS CITY WHO SERVED IN THE WAR'.

There were five nurses serving in the Royal Army Medical Corps, one of whom, Nursing Sister M. J. West, died of disease at Pretoria 20 October 1900. A further twenty-eight served in the RAMC, one of whom died of disease, Corporal F. Cartlidge at Pretoria on 26 January 1902. Eight were enlisted civilian surgeons. The Leeds Corps of the St John's Ambulance sent seventy-seven personnel, two of whom died of disease: Private W. Knight at Bloemfontein on 27 July 1900 and Private T. L. James on 6 June 1901 at Johannesburg.

One of those who signed up with the St John's Ambulance was Lewis Youren who was born in Sheffield in 1881 but soon moved to 31 Barton Terrace, Beeston Hill in Leeds. The Anglo-Boer War website takes up the story:

Youren was assigned to No. 9 General Hospital based in Bloemfontein for most of his service. This hospital was close to a Remount depot, which provided a considerable nuisance in the form of flies. A railway siding in the camp proved most convenient for the reception of patients. As a General Hospital, it had a capacity of 520 beds but within the first week this was exceeded and eventually the daily average tally of patients was 1,400. The influx of patients occurred despite sending about 1,000 convalescents to Base by ambulance train every week. The hospital had a staff complement of 20 medical officers about 20 nursing sisters and 140 orderlies of which, as has been mentioned, Youren was one.

After six months service Youren was discharged on 12 October 1900 and returned to Leeds, but not before he was awarded two medals: 'Queen's South Africa Medal with clasps Cape Colony, Orange Free State and Transvaal to 1169 Ordly. L. Youren, St. John Amb. Bde' and 'St John Ambulance Brigade Medal for the Boer War to 1169 Pte. L. Youren, Leeds Corps'.

NCOs in Youren's unit.

Alfred Atkinson VC

Alfred Atkinson VC (6 February 1874 – 21 February 1900) came from Armley. His father, James Harland Atkinson, was a farrier in the Royal Artillery. Alfred was 26 years old when he died, and a sergeant in the 1st Battalion, The Princess of Wales's Own (Yorkshire Regiment). His valiant action took place on 18 February 1900 during the battle of Paardeberg, for which he was posthumously awarded the VC:

> No. 3264 Sergeant A. Atkinson, Yorkshire Regiment.
> During the battle of Paardeburg, 18th February, 1900, Sergeant A. Atkinson, 1st Battalion Yorkshire Regiment, went out seven times, under heavy and close fire, to obtain water for the wounded. At the seventh attempt he was wounded in the head, and died a few days afterwards.

His Victoria Cross can be seen at the Green Howards Museum, Richmond, Yorkshire.

Leeds Rifles

The Second Boer War saw the Leeds Rifles raise two service companies to support the regular army on campaign. The regiment was accordingly awarded 'South Africa 1900–1902' as its first battle honour. Before that, however, officers from the Leeds Rifles served in Evelyn Wood's Irregular Horse of the Flying Column in the Anglo-Zulu War of 1879.

Yorkshire Hussars (Imperial Yeomanry)

In December 1899, when the decision was made to allow volunteer forces to serve in the Second Boer War, the Imperial Yeomanry was established. The royal warrant required standing yeomanry regiments to provide companies of 115 or so men each for the Imperial Yeomanry. Volunteers from the Yorkshire yeomanry regiments mustered at Sheffield Cavalry Barracks, forming the 9th (Yorkshire (Doncaster)) Company, 3rd Battalion in 1900; 66th (Yorkshire) Company, 16th Battalion (with the Yorkshire Dragoons) in 1900, transferred to the 3rd Battalion in 1900; and the 109th (Yorkshire Hussars) Company, 3rd Battalion in 1901. In January 1901 the original Imperial Yeomanry was formed into the 9th and 11th squadrons, with two additional squadrons, the 109th and 111th. Such was the clamour to join that an additional squadron was formed, the 66th Imperial Yeomanry

Boer guerrillas posing with their Mausers and bandoliers. The lad seated front right is barely in his teens. (photo courtesy David Holt)

Peace day, 1 June 1902, in Briggate.

Squadron, which was then sent to join the 16th Imperial Yeomanry. Overall the first draft of recruits numbered 550 officers, 10,371 men in twenty battalions of four companies each.

The *Yorkshire Evening Post* of 6 January 1900 reported on the Leeds members of the Yorkshire Hussars (Yeomanry) departing the city for training in Sheffield 'amid an exhibition of patriotic fervour perhaps never equalled before in Leeds'. The paper gives a complete list of the troopers, under the command of Captain Gervase Beckett. The announcement of the parade in the City Square 'drew an immense concourse of people thither'. A few days before in its issue of 30 December the *Leeds Mercury* reported that those twenty-six men had passed their medical examination (by a Dr Stott) and had been measured for their khaki uniforms 'as fine a body of men as could be found in the city'. They were expected to sail for South Africa in early January. The list revealed a complete cross-section of Leeds society including medical students, a rag merchant, a vet, a local artist, clerks, a horse trainer and an insurance broker. The Yorkshire Hussars Museum is on the Fulford Road in York.

7. LEEDS AND THE FIRST WORLD WAR

Recruitment

By 4 August 1914 Britain and much of Europe were sucked into a war which would last 1,566 days, cost 8,528,831 lives and 28,938,073 wounded or missing, on both sides. For the most part, news of the outbreak of war that August was greeted in Leeds, as elsewhere, with unbridled enthusiasm to get on with the job and deliver a short sharp shock to the Germans. After all, Christmas was not too far away ...

A First World War infantryman taking aim in the Royal Armouries Museum.

The Hanover Square recruiting office was mobbed, as was the illuminated tram that toured the area urging all able-bodied men of Leeds to join up. Over 800 did, to the tunes of the military band playing on the top deck. Later, after the December 1914 German naval bombardments of Hartlepool, West Hartlepool, Whitby and Scarborough, posters urged the men of Leeds men to 'Remember Scarborough'. Theatre performances and football matches at Elland Road were interrupted to deliver the call; volunteers stood on the pitch to be inspected and applauded. Foreign citizens without naturalization papers were arrested and over fifty Germans were held in the Town Hall and later interned.

Recruitment may well have benefited from the uncertainty of employment hanging over the city. Heavy engineering firms certainly laid off workers, not least global exporter Fowler's who divested themselves of 1,700 workers. By the end of August 1914 8,000 TUC members were out of work. Despite Leeds's healthy contribution to the call-up, the *Yorkshire Post* described the city's response as 'shabby', belying the stories of recruitment centres and trams being besieged and mobbed. The truth of the matter is that a disproportionate number of Leeds men were engaged in essential war work making uniforms, boots, armaments and the like. In any event, how was it that by 16 August both the Leeds Rifles battalions and the Leeds Engineers (Northern Signal Corps) were turning men away?

By the end of September, some 5,000 Leeds men had answered the call, 1,275 of them joining the newly formed Leeds Pals. Leeds was awash with military men.

The recruiting office in City Square.

Leeds Pals recruiting tram, Heaton Park Tramway. A Manchester Corporation Tramways double-decker tram built in 1901, it is now kept at the tramway museum at Heaton Park and was recently decorated as a Leeds Pals recruiting tram for a First World War event in Yorkshire. (© David Dixon and licensed for reuse under Creative Commons Licence)

By August 1915 over 47,000 men had enlisted, chivvied and encouraged by the volunteers from the Leeds Joint Parliamentary Recruiting Committee who paid more than 200,000 visits locally to obtain pledges to join up. Inevitably there were those who sought exemption, so an appeals tribunal was set up in 1916. The vicar of Potternewton was having none of it: he displayed and distributed forms on which were listed for all to see the names and regiments of those who had signed up. Shame, embarrassment, peer pressure and, no doubt, 'encouragement' from spouses, won the day. By the end of the war 82,000 Leeds men had answered the call.

The actual tram – mobbed.

Another motivating force was the Order of the White Feather whose members handed out white feathers to men in the street or posted them through letter boxes. This must have been a dubiously effective tactic, a seriously blunt instrument, to say the least: one Harrogate man committed suicide after receiving his feather.

The euphoria and optimism, however, was short-lived: inexorably mounting casualties saw to that. Food shortages increased, people panic-bought and pushed up the prices, pubs closed early and beer was watered down. The *Yorkshire Post* got the measure of the mood when it told its readers that 'a big section of the public has lost its head completely'. *The Board of Trade Gazette* stated that between July 1914 and June 1917

Leeds University students in the Victoria Hall of the Town Hall compiling the National Register.

21. ALEXANDRIE — Post office street

One of the millions of censored postcards sent by troops from the front to families back home. This one, of Post Office Street, Alexandria, was sent from Harold to his sister Miss Dorothy Todd, 5 The Terrace, Woodhouse Lane, Leeds, on 15 May 1916.

YPRES. — *La Petite Place du Musée avant et après le Bombardement.*
The little Museum place before the Bombardment and after.

A postcard of Ypres before and after the bombardment of 4 March 1917, from Fred to Miss Agnes Dalingwater at 137 Chapeltown Road, Leeds.

This postcard was sent by Len on 16 November 1918 – after the war ended – to his mother Mrs Windross, Prospect, Rawdon, Leeds.

EGYPT. - Ready for a journey.

This postcard from Cairo, again from Harold to Dorothy Todd, 3 October 1916.

the price of fish had gone up 134 per cent, bacon 80 per cent, flour 109 per cent, bread 100 per cent, tea 73 per cent, sugar 178 per cent, milk 60 per cent, butter 67 per cent, salt 66 per cent, cheese 123 per cent, eggs 85 per cent, margarine 68 per cent, potatoes 114 per cent and beef between 87 per cent and 181 per cent depending on the cut. Generally, the average shopping basket had increased in price by 75 per cent over the period.

On the positive side though, allotments increased and parks and golf courses were dug for victory. Hospitals, stately homes and schools were opened up to accept the rising tide of casualties and to provide recuperation; over 57,000 injured troops passed through Leeds. Water supplies at Headingley and Eccup were in the safe hands of Boy Scouts who shared in the guarding of these vital facilities. Twenty amateur wireless stations in Leeds were 'dismantled' in 1914.

Early on in the war Leeds took in and welcomed refugees displaced by the German invasion of Belgium. By the end of October 1914, 800 refugees were in the city, rising to 1,500. Leeds City Art Gallery was used as a reception centre, with 300 people temporarily housed there.

In all, of the 82,000 dispatched to the various theatres of war, 10,000 were killed and many more wounded, often with severe, life-changing disability. Pals regiments had proved a tragic and costly disaster: a mere 500 of the 1,275 Leeds recruits came home again – the economic and social impact alone on the community after 1918 was incalculable. Well-meaning the idea may have been from the donkeys back in HQ, but the ugly words 'cannon fodder' spring to mind with justification when we contemplate the wholesale slaughter of the lions.

University of Leeds Officer Training Corps

University Officer Training Corps (OTCs) was set up to provide instruction for prospective officers in all branches of the army. The Leeds University OTC was raised in September 1909 by Edwin Kitson Clark, a senior officer in the Leeds Rifles, after an appeal to the nation's students from Lord Lucas, the under-secretary of state for war. Cadets participated in drills, musketry, field days, instructional courses, night operations, and annual camps. In 1914 the camp was in full swing on Salisbury Plain, with cadets from Manchester, Birmingham, Bristol, Leeds, Nottingham and Sheffield OTCs, when it was abruptly terminated by the outbreak of war. Leeds OTC was comparatively small with 130 cadets in 1914. However, by March 1915, 239 Leeds cadets had gained commissions and another forty-seven had entered the army as other ranks. Overall 1,596 members of the University served in the war, 290 of whom were killed. Many were highly decorated, including one VC: Captain David Philip Hirsch was awarded the Victoria Cross (Posthumous) for his action when serving with the 4th Yorkshire Regiment in April 1917. Hirsch joined the Leeds University OTC as an extra-mural cadet in December 1914 and was commissioned in March 2015.

Leeds University OTC members queue to sign up in 1914. 1,204 cadets did so during the war.

Leeds women at war

In 1914 approximately 24 per cent of working-age women were already employed, mainly in domestic service jobs, as shop assistants, or doing simple work in small factories. By the end of the war the number of women who had taken up jobs was approximately 1,600,000 – with over a million of those working in munitions factories. The employment which women found open to them throughout the war not only increased, but became diversified, with women doing less of the traditionally female roles they had before the war and taking their place in typically male-dominated areas.

To get as many women into the workforce as quickly as possible, many skilled jobs were (patronizingly) segmented into smaller, simpler tasks, the so-called 'dilution of labour'. The unions opposed this, fearful that this dilution, in addition to the lower levels of pay women earned, would lead to fewer jobs for their male members when they came home from the front. The *Factory Times* magazine in 1916 wrote, 'We must get women back into the home as soon as possible. That they ever left is one of the evil results of the war!'

Munitionettes were paid less than half the rates of male workers; however, striking was made illegal and so there was no recourse to address this. The War Cabinet Committee on Women in Industry claimed to agree with equal pay in principle, but believed that due to their 'lesser strength and special health problems' (unidentified) the output of women was inferior to that of the male workers.

With many of their menfolk – brothers, husbands and fathers – away at the front, the women of Leeds rose to the challenge of stepping into the breach and doing as much as possible to keep the city going: running buses and working as conductors on trams, cleaning trains, filling volatile and toxic shells, clerking in banks and

46

insurance offices, toiling in warehouses and factories – all of these former male bastions fell to girls and women – and these girls and women could hardly be blamed for expecting fairer treatment than they actually got post 1918. For example, during the war there 1,473 women conductors working in Leeds; by October 1919 this fell to sixty-four. The University of Leeds championed the formation of a Voluntary Aid Detachment (VAD) and signed volunteers for concerted sewing, knitting and bandage making.

Wherever and whenever there is war there are victims. Many are male combatants but many more usually are civilians – non-combatants that include women among their number. Women are often left to pick up the pieces during and after war, sometimes literally. Women wait anxiously at home always expecting the worst of bad news; for women, more often than not, their war is not over when the actual war is. Where there is a loss of husband, father or brother they are left to grieve and mourn and to struggle on with their lives, often bringing up young fatherless children. Where the husband-soldier is wounded they may have to spend their new lives as unpaid carers working without state support, tending limbless or otherwise traumatized ex-servicemen, coping with all the grinding physical and psychological issues disabling injury brings. To some extent it has always been thus, and to some extent it still is today.

Nevertheless, the First World War did present employment and opportunities for career advancement for some, mainly middle- and upper-class women. Teaching experience was easier to come by as was postgraduate research work in university cities like Leeds. Women with scientific backgrounds suddenly found themselves in demand and were employed in industrial scientific laboratories, not least in munitions research. A former Leeds university student, May Sybil Burr (née Leslie), who graduated in 1906 became the chemist in charge of the munitions factory in Liverpool in 1916 and was awarded a doctorate by the University of Leeds for her research on explosives, which had included confidential wartime investigations.

The Faculty of Technology at Leeds ran classes at the Central Technical School, Cockburn High School and at other schools to train women up to take in semi-skilled work at munitions factories.

Isabella Ford

Isabella Ormston Ford (1855–1924) was a social reformer, suffragist and writer on socialism, feminism and workers' rights. She was born in Adel Grange in Adel, the youngest of eight children in a pacifist Quaker family. Ford felt compelled to resign from the National Union of Women's Suffrage Societies over the vexed issue of their support for the war. She then concentrated on working toward peace and founded the Leeds branch of the Women's Peace Crusade.

Leonora Cohen OBE

One of Leeds's most active women's champions was Leonora Cohen. Cohen (1873–1978) was a housewife and suffragette from Leeds; she gained fame in 1913 when she tried to smash the glass showcase in the Tower of London Jewel House which contained the insignia of the Order of Merit. A note wrapped around the iron bar she used read: 'This is my protest against the Government's treachery to the working women of Great Britain.' On this occasion she was wrestled to the ground by Beefeaters.

She was arrested on several more occasions and once went on a hunger and then a thirst strike while in custody in Armley Gaol. She was an active militant, organizing protest marches on Woodhouse and Hunslet moors. A photograph now in the Leeds City Archive was among her papers and bears the annotation in her handwriting: 'I, Leonora Cohen was arrested and charged with inciting the public to militancy under Edward 3rds act ("a trumped-up false charge") at the same period as George Lansbury and John Scurr. A protest meeting was held in Trafalgar Square, London for the release of the three charged, under the old Antediluvian Act.'

Leonora was born in 1873 in Hunslet. At 14, she was apprenticed to a city centre milliner working, as women were required to do, long hours without pay until she was upgraded to a probationer, paid 2s 6d a week. By 16, she was promoted to head milliner and in her mid-twenties graduated to becoming a millinery buyer in Bridlington, where in 1900 she married jeweller Henry Cohen, much to the dismay of both families.

In 1911 Leonora was secretary of the Leeds branch of the militant Women's Social and Political Union. A demonstration in London which ended in window-smashing and stone-throwing saw Leonora incarcerated in Holloway for seven days.

The Tower of London incident followed: she was so nervous before the attack that she went twice round on the Circle Line before entering the Tower. Afterwards, Leonora was put on trial but acquitted on a technicality. Back in Leeds, Asquith's visit in November 1913 was incendiary: two suffragettes tried to set fire to the Headingley football stand, and violent demonstrations simmered around the Hippodrome where Asquith was to speak. Leonora was arrested for smashing windows and was sent to Armley Gaol. Hostilities were put on hold for the duration of the war, and in February 1918 women over 30 were finally given the vote – better than nothing for the sterling support the women of Britain gave the country in its years of need. Women, however, had to wait another ten years before they finally gained full voting equality with men.

By 1923, Cohen had become the first woman president of the Yorkshire Federation of Trade Councils that she served for twenty-five years. Her former house in Clarendon Road is marked by a blue plaque, and in 1928 she was awarded an OBE; she served as a Leeds magistrate for over thirty years. Leonora Cohen died at the age of 105.

Flora Lion

Flora Lion (1878–1958), a celebrated English portrait painter, was commissioned by the Ministry of Information to paint factory scenes on the home front. The ministry issued

The Leeds flying-boats.

her permits to set up her easel in factories in Leeds and Bradford. In Leeds she sketched scenes in a factory building wooden flying-boats. In Bradford, Lion painted women working in a munitions factory. Both paintings were finished in 1918 by which time the Ministry of Information had unfortunately been wound up and the Imperial War Museum had taken over the MoI artists' scheme. Sadly, the IWM had no funds available to purchase new artworks, and so could not accept Lion's paintings despite her offering them at only 150 guineas each. Lion was also one of three women artists, alongside Anna Airy and Dorothy Coke, considered for commissions by the British War Memorials Committee but this came to nothing.

Dorothy Una Ratcliffe

A bronze in the City Museum celebrates Dorothy Una Ratcliffe (1887–1967), niece of Lord Brotherton and writer of poetry, some in Yorkshire dialect. She is one of the celebrated but often overlooked women poets of the First World War and helped Lord Brotherton equip the Leeds Old Pals Regiment; she also assisted with Belgian refugees making good use of her facility with French. Dorothy Una Ratcliffe (often known as D.U.R.) was a flamboyant socialite and something of a bohemian who loved the natural world, published nearly fifty books, travelled the world, nurtured her garden and loved Yorkshire and the Dales in particular. She was raised in Sussex and Surrey and in 1909, aged 22, she married Charles Frederick Ratcliffe, nephew and heir of the wealthy chemical tycoon Edward Allen Brotherton, later Lord Brotherton of Wakefield. The newlyweds moved into a house near Edward Brotherton's home at Roundhay Hall.

A bronze in the City Museum of Dorothy Una Ratcliffe.

Armistice

There was palpable dismay and disgruntlement among the returning troops, the heroes: Leeds's veterans' units returned to the city in dribs and drabs. While the people who had been left at home had enjoyed fireworks and convivial and joyous street parties, the piecemeal return of troops was often a more melancholy, downbeat affair. Over 40,000 celebrated outside the Town Hall but the returning heroes would witness little of what the *Yorkshire Post* reported: 'the city was alive with shouting, singing, merry-making crowds ... the glare of fireworks and bonfires in the suburbs added to the gaiety of a great day'. Just one example is Arthur Pearson, a Leeds Pal who served right throughout the war, notably as a stretcher bearer at the battle of the Somme, and who went on to become a signaller. He was demobbed in Whitley Bay and returned to Leeds with no crowds to greet him. He was back at work in two days.

Leeds regiments in the Great War

Leeds Bantams: The West Yorkshire Regiment (Prince of Wales's Own), 17th Service Battalion (2nd Leeds)

Bantam units were formed as a response to the need for ever more men on the front lines. The Member of Parliament for Birkenhead, Alfred Bigland, gained permission from the War Office to form a battalion of men who were under regulation height of 5 foot 3 inches but otherwise fit for active service. The Bantam units were recruited from industrial and coal-mining areas where short stature was a positive advantage and men were used to hard, physical labour. Height, though, for Bantams still had to be a minimum of 5 feet. Many of these Bantams were especially suited for tunnelling. It was not long before 3,000 men had volunteered. The original volunteers were formed into the 1st and 2nd Birkenhead battalions of the Cheshire Regiment followed by Bantam units in the Lancashire Fusiliers, West Yorkshires, Royal Scots, and Highland Light Infantry.

On 8 December 1914 the Lord Mayor of Leeds raised a Bantam battalion of the West Yorkshire Regiment, the 17th (Service) Battalion, also known as the 2nd Leeds Pals. The usual enthusiasm to join up followed with most of the recruits being shepherds, miners and woollen workers from the mills of Leeds and Bradford and other textile towns. At first, drill took place on Holbeck Moor.

After initial training without equipment or uniform, the division was formed in Yorkshire with headquarters at Masham, in June 1915. The 17th West Yorkshires 2nd Leeds Bantams were billeted at Ilkley from January to May 1915. The proximity of home to their billets proved too strong a temptation for a number of Leeds Bantams who were caught 'extending their leave' or leaving barracks without permission. In August, the Bantams moved to Salisbury Plain. In late 1915, orders were received to move to Egypt, but this changed and after further training at Masham, the Bantams left for France in July 1916, cutting their teeth on the Somme. By 1917, the Bantams had been subsumed by the senior Leeds Service Battalion, the 15th West Yorkshires.

At the battle of the Somme, the 17th Battalion West Yorkshires suffered shocking losses with over a quarter of them killed. However, Bantams had a reputation for punching well above their weight and the Leeds Bantams were awarded one Victoria Cross, a Distinguished Service Order, three Military Crosses, twenty-four Military Medals and Distinguished Conduct Medals.

The regiment participated in the following actions: the battle of Albert, 1916, including the capture of Montauban, Mametz, Fricourt, Contalmaison and La Boisselle; the battle of Bazentin Ridge, Arrow Head Copse and Maltz Horn Farm, the fighting for Falfemont Farm; the German retreat to the Hindenburg Line in April 1917; the fighting in Houthulst Forest; the second battle of Passchendaele in November 1917; the first battle of Bapaume in March 1918; the fourth battle of Ypres, September–October 1918; the battle of Courtrai and actions at Tieghem.

Yorkshire Hussars

As the 1/1st Yorkshire Hussars, the regiment had its headquarters in York, with the squadrons based thus: A Squadron in Leeds under Major F. H. Fawkes, B Squadron in York, C Squadron in Knaresborough and D Squadron in Middlesbrough. They were mobilized on 5 August 1914, and the men assembled at their squadron headquarters where they were issued with horses and infantry rifles but not swords. Over the next two days they took up positions along the east coast of Yorkshire with the HQ at Scarborough.

Later in August the Foreign Service Regiment was formed from volunteers plus recruits. This was later called the 1/1st Yorkshire Hussars, commanded by Lieutenant-Colonel Viscount Helmsley, wintering in Harlow, Essex. From April 1915, the regiment was split between three different divisions, to provide cavalry support: HQ and A Squadron were placed under the command of 50th (Northumbrian) Division and sent to Le Havre on 18 April 1915. A Squadron saw action at the second battle of Ypres the very next day after disembarkation, under the command of Major G. R. Lane Fox.

From 22 to 25 May they were in a dismounted role on the Menin Road where they took ten casualties, five killed and five wounded, including Major Lane Fox. June and July saw them in the Bailleul–Hazebrouk area providing digging parties and performing policing duties. In May 1916, the regiment was reconstituted and placed under the command of XVII Corps, based at Gouy-en-Ternois as the Corps Cavalry Regiment, and seeing action at the battle of Arras under Lieutenant-Colonel W. Pepys. They later moved to Berles, between Arras and St Pol, where they stayed for over a year.

In August 1917 the regiment was converted to infantry and deployed to Etaples for infantry training. In October 1917, 400 or so men were dispatched to the 9th (Service) Battalion of the West Yorkshire Regiment, which was renamed the 9th (Yorkshire Hussars Yeomanry) Battalion. They wore the Yorkshire Hussars cap badge and West York collar badges. They fought at Passchendale north of Lens and then carried out a successful raid on the Norman Brickstacks.

The battalion wintered in the miserable colliery district south of Bethune. They held the sector opposite Hulluch and Haisnes through spring 1918 and endured gas shelling, first on 9 April and on ensuing days at St Elie. On 15 June they raided the Hairpin Craters at St Elie in which a tunnel was successfully blown up by Second Lieutenant A. Dalley. On 24 August they were deployed to Arras for the final push, losing two killed and six wounded east of Pelves; as consolation of a kind they captured a German clothing store. Their final action of the war was at Roisin where they were exposed to shelling in a sunken road. They lost five officers and twelve other ranks killed, and two officers and fifty other ranks wounded, with a further forty-four missing. The Hussars sustained forty-three more casualties the next day when the Germans shelled Roisin.

In 1919 the regiment was repurposed as horsed cavalry under Lieutenant-Colonel G. R. Lane Fox. In the reforming of the Territorial Army the fourteen senior regiments of yeomanry were armed as cavalry with rifles and swords and with Vickers and Hotchkiss machine guns. The first post-war camp was at Harrogate where horses were hired from a farmer or else officers and men provided their own especially in the country troops such as Helmsley and Easingwold. The three squadrons were based at Leeds, Middlesbrough and York, with the HQ at York.

Leeds Rifles, The Prince of Wales's Own Regiment of Yorkshire (TA)

We have already noted how in 1908 the Volunteer Force became the Territorial Force and was expanded to form two 1,000-men-strong battalions: the 7th and 8th (Leeds Rifles) battalions, The Prince of Wales's Own (West Yorkshire Regiment) (TA). It comprised three infantry brigades and was equipped with artillery, engineers, transport, medical services – everything it needed to fight a war, as part of the 1st West Riding Infantry Brigade (TF).

In July 1914 both Leeds Rifles battalions returned early from camp at Scarborough with orders to prepare for war. So great was the response that two second-line battalions were formed. The original battalions were identified as 1/7th and 1/8th, the two second-line as the 2/7th and 2/8th. The first-line battalions served in France and Flanders from April 1915, continuously through to the end of the war. Along with the second-line units formed by the West Riding Division, these two battalions became part of the 62nd (2nd West Riding) Infantry Division (TF) and their brigade became 185th (2/1st West Riding) Infantry Brigade (TF).

The Leeds Rifles at Carlton Hill Barracks.

Much of their active service involved holding the infamous Ypres Salient as well fighting at the Somme, Passchendaele and in the final victory push.

The 62nd (2nd West Riding) Infantry Division was an all-territorial division which began active service in January 1917 and quickly established for itself a reputation as a formidable assault division. The 185th Brigade was tasked with recapturing the recently lost French front line at Bligny Ridge. Within an hour of the attack starting on 20 July, the assault was held up: forty-three Leeds riflemen were killed and 219 wounded or missing for little gain. The 8th Battalion (Leeds Rifles) attacked again on 28 July. Losses were fourteen killed, ninety-six wounded and eleven missing. On the plus side the battalion took sixty-nine prisoners, nine machine guns, as well as the tactically critical Bligny Ridge. The 8th Battalion was awarded the prestigious French Croix de Guerre avec Palme en Bronze for its gallantry in capturing Bligny Ridge. Thenceforth all members of the Leeds Rifles were entitled to wear the ribbon of the Croix de Guerre.

All told, about 2,050 soldiers of the Leeds Rifles died on active service in France and Flanders between 1915 and 1918.

After the war, the 7th and 8th Leeds Rifles were both reconstituted in the Territorial Army and continued to serve as part of the 146th (1st West Riding) Infantry Brigade of the 49th (West Riding) Infantry Division. The 7th Battalion was commanded by Lieutenant-Colonel Charles Herbert Tetley, who had won a DSO during the war; his cousin James Noel Tetley was a junior officer.

As another war loomed, 1936 saw the 8th (Leeds Rifles) Battalion transferred to the Royal Artillery, converted to the anti-aircraft (AA) role as 66th (Leeds Rifles, The West Yorkshire Regiment) Anti-Aircraft Brigade, forming part of 31st (North Midland) Anti-Aircraft Group. Their job was to defend West Yorkshire as part of 2nd Anti-Aircraft Division.

In April 1938 the 7th (Leeds Rifles) Battalion converted to the armoured role as 45th (Leeds Rifles) Battalion, Royal Tank Regiment. In June 1939, the company at Morley was hived off to form the cadre for a duplicate unit, the 51st (Leeds Rifles) Battalion, Royal Tank Regiment. During the Munich Crisis the TA's AA units were mobilized on 23 September 1938; they were stood down on 13 October. On 24 August, ahead of the declaration of war, AA Command was fully mobilized.

1st (Leeds) Yorkshire West Riding Artillery Volunteer Corps

During the war the three West Riding brigades were part of the 49th (West Riding) Division, sailing for France in 1915. Each formed a second-line brigade in 1915 (2/1st and 2/2nd West Riding Brigade RFA (TF) respectively), in support of the 62nd Division. In May 1916 the brigades were redesignated 245th, 246th and 247th brigades Royal Field Artillery (TF).

The Doncaster-based West Riding Divisional Army Service Corps parading in Park Row, 28 April 1915. Note the new recruits marching without uniforms. The corps provided horse and motor transport; they left for France the next day.

After the war, the names of the brigades were changed back to their pre-war designations of 1st, 2nd and 3rd West Riding brigades RFA when they were re-formed into the Territorial Army in 1920 at Leeds and Bradford. This was only to last a year when in 1921 they were renamed yet again, this time as the 69th and 70th (West Riding) brigades Royal Field Artillery (Territorial Army). In 1939, the 69th formed a second-line regiment at Bramley, 121st Field Regiment RA (TA); the 70th likewise formed 122nd Field Regiment RA (TA) in Bradford. Motor vehicles replaced horses.

The Prince of Wales's Own (West Yorkshire Regiment)

During the war the regiment made a significant impact: it raised thirty-five battalions, was awarded fifty-seven battle honours and four Victoria Crosses. Sadly, however, this came at a dreadful cost with the loss of 12,700 men during the war. Here are the movements of the various Leeds battalions between 1914 and 1918:

1/5th 1/6th & 1/7th battalions Territorial Force

On 4 August 1914 the 1/5th was stationed at York, the 1/6th at Bradford and the 1/7th at Leeds, as part of the 1st West Riding Brigade of the West Riding Division. All three then moved to Selby and back to York via Strensall Camp. In March 1915 they moved to Gainsborough, mobilized for war and landed at Boulogne. In May they became the 146th Brigade of the 49th Division that saw action in 1915 at the battle of Aubers Ridge which saw the first phosgene gas attack. 1916 ushered in the battles of Albert, Bazentin Ridge, Pozieres Ridge and Flers-Courcelette. 1917 saw operations on the Flanders coast and the battle of Poelcapelle. In 1918 they fought at the battles of Estaires, Messines, Bailleul, the first and second battles of Kemmel Ridge and the battles of the Scherpenberg, the Selle and Valenciennes.

1/8th Battalion (Leeds Rifles) Territorial Force

Much the same activity as 1/5th 1/6th & 1/7th battalions Territorial Force. In August 1914 they were stationed at Leeds and as part of the 1st West Riding Brigade of the West Riding Division before moving to Selby, then Strensall and back to York. In March 1915 they moved to Gainsborough, prepared for war and landed at Boulogne. Their various actions on the Western Front are dealt with above, alongside the 1/5th 1/6th & 1/7th battalions.

2/7th & 2/8th battalions Territorial Force

Formed at Leeds in September 1914 then moved to Matlock to join the 185th Brigade of the 62nd Division. The following May they moved to Thoresby Park, then Retford and then Newcastle. In January 1916 they were on Salisbury Plain and a year later mobilized for war and landed at Le Havre. 1917 saw them in action with operations on the Ancre, the German retreat to the Hindenburg Line, the first attack on Bullecourt, fighting the German attack on Lagnicourt, and the Cambrai operations. 1918 included the battle of

Bapaume and the second battle of Arras. In June 1918 they were swallowed up by the 18th Battalion of the York & Lancaster Regiment at Brighton.

3/7th & 3/8th battalions Territorial Force
Formed at Leeds in March 1915; in April 1916 they were in Clipstone and became the 7th and 8th reserve battalions. That September the 8th absorbed the 7th as part of the West Riding Reserve Brigade Territorial Force. Autumn 1917 saw them in Rugeley, Cannock Chase. The following year they were posted to Clonmaney, County Donegal as part of the 27th Reserve Brigade.

5th (Service) Battalion (1st Leeds)
Formed in Leeds in September 1914 by the Lord Mayor and the City of Leeds, before moving to Colsterdale near Masham for training. In June 1915 they moved over to nearby Ripon and joined the 93rd Brigade of the 31st Division. In August 1915 they moved to Fovant, Salisbury Plain. That December they sailed to Egypt to defend a section on the Suez Canal. March 1916 saw them deployed to the Western Front where they fought in various actions, including the battles of Albert and the Ancre; in 1917 the third battle of the Scarpe and the capture of Oppy Wood. In December they amalgamated with the 17th Battalion to form the 15/17th Battalion. 1918 saw them fight the battles of St Quentin and Bapaume, the second battle of Arras, and the battles of Estaires and Hazebrouck, the defence of Nieppe Forest, the attack at La Becque, the capture of Vieux Berquin, the fourth battle of Ypres and the action at Tieghem.

17th (Service) Battalion (2nd Leeds)
This Bantam battalion has been covered in the earlier section on Leeds Bantams: The West Yorkshire Regiment (Prince of Wales's Own), 17th Service Battalion (2nd Leeds).

21st (Service) Battalion (Wool Textile Pioneers)
This unit was formed in September 1915 across the West Riding (especially Halifax) by the Lord Mayor and the City of Leeds. In February 1916 they were in training at Skipton's Raikeswood Camp having undertaken initial training in Halifax. In June 1916 the battalion was mobilized for war and landed in France, joining the 4th Division as a pioneer battalion with whom it fought on the Somme offensive. Other actions included the battle of Arras, the first and third battles of the Scarpe, the third battle of Ypres, where they fought in the battle of Polygon Wood, the battle of Broodseinde, the battle of Poelcapelle and the first battle of Passchendaele. In 1918 they were involved on the Somme, then returned to Flanders fighting in the defence of Hinges Ridge during the battle of Hazebrouck and then the battle of Bethune, the advance in Flanders, the second battles of Arras, the battles of the Hindenburg Line and the final advance in Picardy. Some historians consider the Wool Textile Pioneers as a Pals battalion.

Volunteers generally had to buy their own uniforms; they carried out night patrols around the city, guarded waterworks and railway lines. The RASC Motor Transport Volunteers commandeered private cars and ambulances, using them to ferry wounded servicemen from the railway stations to hospitals in the city and to convey soldiers home on leave to outlying towns and villages.

Above: Leeds Volunteer Battalions camp at Monk Fryston, Whitsun 1915.

Below: Messengers and signallers of the Leeds Volunteer Battalions.

PT at Leeds Volunteer Battalions camp at Monk Fryston, Whitsun 1915.

15th Battalion (1st Leeds), The Prince of Wales's Own (West Yorkshire Regiment) – The Leeds Pals

Nothing illustrates better the tragedy of war and the devastating effect it can have on a community back home than the ill-conceived though well-intentioned concept of the so-called Pals battalions. The belief among the military gurus was that fighting shoulder to shoulder with your mates would foster a unique morale-boosting camaraderie that would produce a fighting force second to none. That patently was not the case. Pals was something of a northern thing although they were raised all over England, Wales, Scotland and Northern Ireland: there were Pals battalions from Edinburgh, Glasgow Manchester, Oldham, Liverpool, Hull, Grimsby, Ripon, Catterick, Barnsley, Tees-side, Newcastle, Bradford, and Leeds to name just a few. They were not always regionally based: there were Pals battalions known as Public Schools Pals, Miners, Public Works Pioneers, Church Lads, Footballers, British Empire League, Empire, North Eastern Railwaymen, Frontiersmen, Sportsman's, Bankers, West Ham Utd Supporters and Arts & Crafts.

Pals battalions were crucial in the call to arms for Kitchener's New Army. Between September 1914 and June 1916, 351 infantry battalions were raised by the War Office through the traditional channels and a further 643 battalions were raised locally.

Hundreds of men from diverse, but selective, walks of life signed up at Leeds Town Hall in September 1914. White collar workers predominated and many were university educated, or celebrity sportsmen. These bizarre qualifications inevitably led to a number of keen applicants being turned away, one example being a clerk, E. Robinson, who was rejected because his father was a farm labourer. The English class system was alive and well, impervious to the knowledge that German bullets and shrapnel did not make such fatuous discriminations. E. Robinson joined the Royal Artillery on the same day; history does not record any comment he may have made.

By 8 September 1,275 men had enlisted and passed their medicals; the final number of 'Leeds Pals' later exceeded 2,000 of whom only about 500 survived. The average age was 20 to 21. Theoretically at least there was a requirement for education and intelligence among the recruits. In Leeds's case a number of famous sportsmen also made the grade including footballers Evelyn Lintott, a Leeds City and England international, and Morris Flemming; Yorkshire cricketers included Major Booth, wicket-keeper Arthur Dolphin and Roy Kilner; athletes such as Albert Gutteridge and George Colcroft were included.

The recruits left Leeds for basic training in two detachments, on 22 and 25 September to jubilant send-offs at Leeds station by crowds of some 20,000. Training was at Colsterdale near Masham; land at Breary Banks had been placed at

Pipes aplenty but not a uniform in sight.

the battalion's disposal by the city's waterworks department. The speed and alacrity which accompanied the recruitment campaign caught the authorities by surprise. Ben Wade, the Leeds pipemaker, donated pipes and an ounce of Tetley's 'Golden Pelican' tobacco, but their uniforms did not arrive until November. Members of the public donated blankets.

But it was not all jubilation, as the *Leeds and District Weekly Citizen* of 20 October 1914 reported: 'It was the cheering that killed recruiting in Leeds.' Twenty thousand had cheered Leeds Pals off at the station but the unit had turned away numerous artisans '& 90 per cent of Leeds recruits left without a cheer & without a song ... The boom over the "Pals" was all very nice & full of esteem & goodwill but it froze the stream of recruits right off.' Snobbery was alive and well. Two proposed workers' battalions failed to attract sufficient recruits as the local economy improved.

The first colonel of the 15th (Service) Battalion West Yorkshire Regiment was Walter Stead, local solicitor and member of the council; it was he who filed the application to Lord Kitchener for permission to raise the Leeds Pals. This was supported by a telegram to Kitchener from Leeds's mayor, Edward Brotherton, who stood the cost of raising and equipping the battalion. He even went further in his generosity when he deposited his personal fortune with the council to offset any future expense the city might incur in maintaining the Pals.

Unloading supplies at Colsterdale, September 1914.

Leeds Pals relaxing with tea at Headingley, 1 June 1915.

Initially, tents were the main form of accommodation; the only permanent billets were the water-workmen's huts and a small bungalow used by officers. Ironically, there was no piped water on site and the men had to wash and shave in a small stream nearby.

In June 1915 the Pals decamped to North Camp at Ripon to join the 1st and 2nd Bradford Pals and the 18th Durham Light Infantry for brigade training, then south to Fovant Military Camp, overseas to Egypt and later to France and the Somme.

An inevitable consequence in December 1915 when the British and their allies evacuated the Gallipoli peninsula was that significant numbers of Turkish troops would be freed up to fight elsewhere. The Suez Canal was an obvious target so the British set about strengthening the canal defences. France had been considered the initial deployment for the Leeds Pals but that all changed when the transport section of 102 men left Devonport on 6 December on board HMS *Shropshire*, Egypt bound. The rest of the battalion, along with their pioneers from the 12th King's Own Yorkshire Light Infantry and Army Service Corps followed from Liverpool along with the 6,000 troops from the rest of 93rd Brigade on board the converted liner, the RMS *Empress of Britain* on 7 December. The *Shropshire* docked at Port Said on 20 December 1915, the *Empress* on the 21st. Sadly, the ship carrying beer from Leeds was sunk en route.

The Turkish threat never materialized, so on 1 March the battalion boarded the troopship HMT *Asconia* bound for France and then on to the Somme. The breathtaking ineptitude exhibited by the military strategists which led to the carnage that started at 7.09 a.m. on 1 July 1916 is well documented, as is the abject failure of the two-week barrage preceding the attack. Suffice to say that of the 58,000 or so casualties, 20,000 men were killed. On that day, the British army lost fifteen men killed and thirty wounded every minute for twenty-four hours.

The 750 Leeds Pals who fought that day as part of the 31st Division sustained, in the few minutes after Zero Hour at 7.30 a.m., casualties of twenty-four officers and 504 other ranks. Of these thirteen officers were killed, with two more later dying of wounds, and 209 other ranks killed with twenty-four more dying of wounds. Apparently, every street in Leeds lost at least one man as the Pals went over the top.

Private Morrison Fleming was one of the Leeds Pals injured that day. He wrote: 'The whistle blew and over we went. One or two of our lads had dropped down, they were dropping all round us, and one that had dropped was screaming out, his leg was in a [bad] way ... I could see the bodies going up in the air. A terrible sight, a sight that I'll never forget, and the ground was just like an upheaval, one mass of flame everywhere.'

At Serre the Leeds Pals advanced from some copses which happened to be named after the four Gospels. The battalion had been softened up by German shelling in its trenches before Zero Hour and when it went over the top, it was met by waves of deadly machine-gun fire. A small number of men reached the German barbed wire. Later that morning the Germans came out from their trenches to clear the bodies off the wire, killing any still alive.

Private A. V. Pearson, Leeds Pals: 'The name of Serre and the date of 1st July is engraved deep in our hearts, along with the faces of our "Pals", a grand crowd of chaps. We were two years in the making and ten minutes in the destroying.'

After the war, the Leeds Pals Association was founded in 1919 for original Colsterdale men. In 1935 a memorial cairn was set up at Colsterdale to which the Pals Association returns each year to place a wreath. Armistice Day each year sees the Pals' descendants laying a wreath on Leeds cenotaph. A full alphabetical list of Leeds Pals can be found at https://leedspalsvolunteerresearchers.wordpress.com/alphabetical-list-of-pals/

Jogendra Sen

One Pal was Jogendra Sen, a highly educated, multilingual Bengali who graduated in electrical engineering at the University of Leeds in 1913; he was one of the first to sign up to the 1st Leeds 'Pals' Battalion in September 1914. Jogendra remains the only known non-white soldier to serve with the 15th West Yorkshire Regiment during the war. Despite his education and intellect, he was rejected as an officer and did not progress beyond the rank of private. So very British. Jogendra was killed in action at Bus-Les-Artois in the Somme department: he was part of a wiring party that was bombarded late on the night of 22 May 1916 and after being hit by shrapnel in the leg and neck, the Bengali succumbed to his wounds. Private Sen's name can be seen on the university's war memorial in the Brotherton Library entrance hall. In total, India contributed some 1.5 million men as soldiers and non-combatants, including labourers and porters, to the war. Dr Santanu Das, reader in English at King's College London and an expert on India's involvement in the First World War, paid a visit in 2005 to Sen's home town of Chandernagore – a former French colony. There Dr Das saw Sen's bloodstained glasses in a display case in the town's museum, the Institut de Chandernagore. He said: 'I was absolutely stunned when I saw the pair of glasses. It's one of the most poignant artefacts I've seen – a mute witness to the final moments of Sen's life. It was astonishing that something so fragile has survived when almost everything else has perished.'

Royal Artillery: 210th, 211th and 223rd Field Artillery – (Leeds) Field Companies

In early 1915 Leeds was the recruiting ground for two field companies of Royal Engineers – the 210th and 211th Field Artillery, made up of 600 men in total. At the end of March they were sent to Ilkley for training. More recruitment in Leeds followed in May 1915 with the formation of the 223rd Field Company and the 31st Divisional Signals Company, adding another 600 troops to form part of the 31st Division. A shortage of horses for use in the engineers' training was eased by importing forty mules from the Argentine. The 15th Battalion, The West Yorkshire Regiment (1st Leeds Pals) was also part of the division.

Imperial Cadet Yeomanry

In August 1916 Ilkley was also home to 200 boys of the Leeds and Bradford detachments of Imperial Cadet Yeomanry, a Territorial Army unit of the Officer Training Corps attached to the Yorkshire Hussars. The average age was fourteen. The following summer, 150 more attended a territorial cadet training camp, some of whom were from Leeds Modern School.

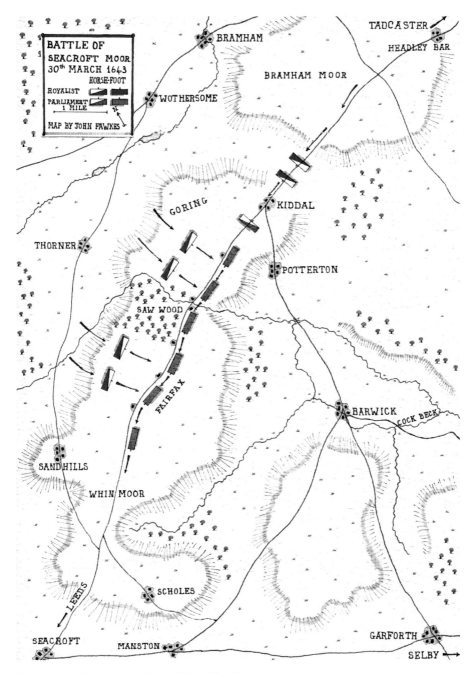

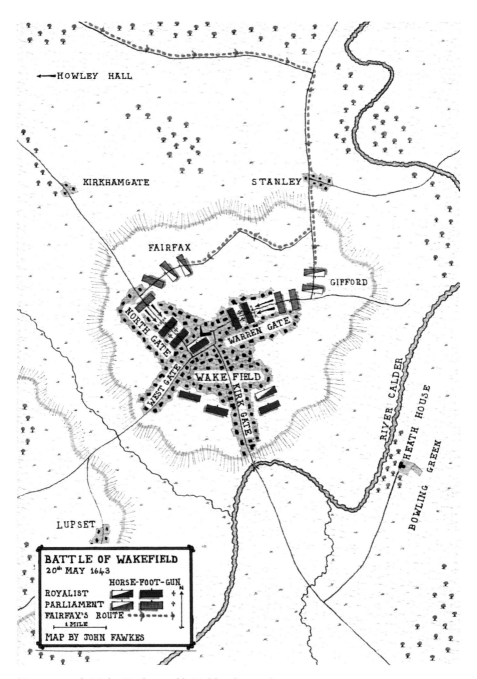

← HOWLEY HALL

KIRKHAMGATE

STANLEY

FAIRFAX

GIFFORD

NORTH GATE

WARREN GATE

WEST GATE

WAKEFIELD

KIRK GATE

RIVER CALDER

HEATH HOUSE

BOWLING GREEN

LUPSET

BATTLE OF WAKEFIELD
20th MAY 1643
HORSE-FOOT-GUN
ROYALIST
PARLIAMENT
FAIRFAX'S ROUTE
¼ MILE
MAP BY JOHN FAWKES

(Courtesy and © John Fawkes and britishbattles.com)

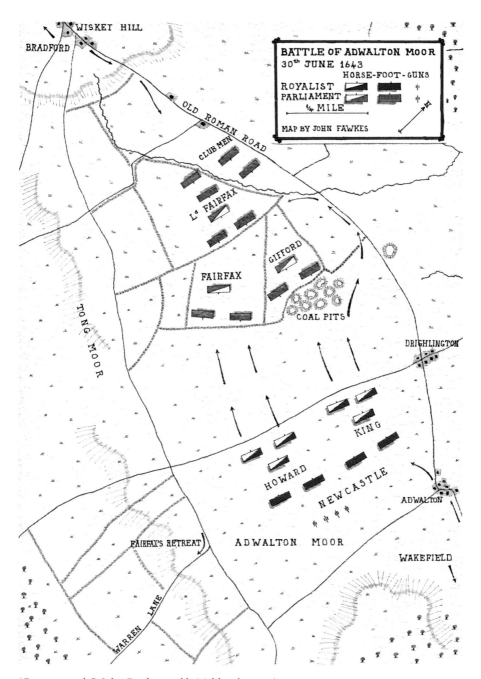

A Parliamentary soldier in the Royal Armouries Museum.

A Great War recruitment poster urging footballers to join the Football Pals.

'In the trenches' – an Anglo-French concord postcard sent to Mrs MacFarlane at 16 Azalea Street off Beckett Street, Leeds on 23 May 191?. Millions of postcards were sent home from the fronts in the Great War.

The Great War: a munitions worker recruitment poster invoking patriotism with an attempt to introduce a touch of glamour into work that was anything but glamorous.

A Leeds TUC poster promoting the celebration of the centenary of the Leeds Convention.

Leeds Royal Engineers, 210th Field Company in Regent Road, Ilkley, March 1915.

Apart from Gibraltar and Carlton barracks, the Old Eccentric Club in Albion Street was also used as a barracks. Men signed up to join the Special Constabulary and women the Voluntary Women's Patrols. At their height the Specials had 2,086 constables. Crime in the city fell. The Leeds auxiliary fire brigade could call on ninety-seven men. During the war Elland Road was used for drill and shooting practice. The terrace behind the goal at the north end was known as the Spion Kop, or Kop, named after the famous hill in South Africa where 322 British soldiers lost their lives in January 1900, during the Second Boer War. The ground was also requisitioned by the War Office during the Second World War.

Medical Services

The appalling injuries inflicted throughout led to enormous strides being made in areas of medicine such as infection control, dental, oral and maxillofacial surgery, burns and plastic surgery, trauma, orthopaedic surgery, orthotics and prosthetics, physio- and occupational therapy and post-trauma psychiatric issues. Leeds was among the cities making those strides with its hospitals and the medical school at the university. Medical care, surgery, nursing and rehabilitation were catered for in a range of hospitals: pre-existing military hospitals, Territorial Force (TF) hospitals which had been used for training pre-war and were fully mobilized in 1914, pre-war asylums and public hospitals taken over for military use and auxiliary or voluntary hospitals. Military hospitals were clinical and surgical, auxiliary more convalescent and rehabilitation.

East Leeds Military Hospital, Beckett Street

17 September 1914 was a pivotal day for Leeds. That was the day on which the first convoy of eighty wounded soldiers arrived back in their home city at the old Midland Station; they were casualties from the battle of the Marne; few of them were able to walk and many sported injuries too terrible to describe. A sombre crowd of 6,000 or so Leeds people looked on as the soldiers were taken from the City Square to Beckett's Park. They showered the troops with cigarettes and tobacco.

The old Leeds Union Workhouse in Beckett Street (later, in 1925, St James's Hospital) had been converted in 1915 into a 500-bed hospital for just that 17 September eventuality and rebadged the East Leeds Military, or War, Hospital. There was a branch hospital at Killingbeck and medical facilities at Gledhow Hall, and at Harehills Council School. With No. 2 Northern General, it treated over 57,000 patients throughout the war. After 1917, East Leeds took on the administrative role originally based at Beckett's Park; it was also the first specialist dental unit in the country. Dentures for the entire Northern Command were fitted here and new methods in oral surgery and jaw reconstruction were developed.

Leeds Union Workhouse from the cemetery – the last resting place of many paupers.
(© St James's Hospital, Leeds)

No. 2 Northern General, Beckett's Park

The No. 2 Northern Hospital in Leeds had affiliated hospitals in Harrogate, Cookridge, Lotherton Hall, Armley, Stokesley, Northallerton and Thirsk. It was a Territorial Force hospital based in the converted teacher training college, City of Leeds Training College, at Beckett's Park. Awaiting the first casualties were 600 beds and ninety-two nurses.

Northern General was the UK's largest special surgical hospital for orthopaedics, performing nerve suture, or 'stitching', procedures as well as large-scale bone grafting. Paraffin baths were first used at Beckett's Park as preparation for massage and electric treatment. Electro-shock therapy was also administered to assist post-surgical nerve regrowth as well as the retraining of muscles. Surgeons and doctors from all over the country came to observe this treatment and be educated.

Beckett's Park pioneered occupational therapy with its Curative Workshop, one of the key foundations of the treatment of disabled servicemen. The aim, of course, was to train disabled men to adapt to and support themselves in civilian and domestic life. There were classes on splint-making, basket-making, weaving, blacksmith's work, tailoring, short-hand and typing, shoe-making, and needlecraft.

The Grand Duchess George of Russia opened the YMCA recreation hall on campus in 1915, complete with cinema equipment and facilities for concerts, lectures,

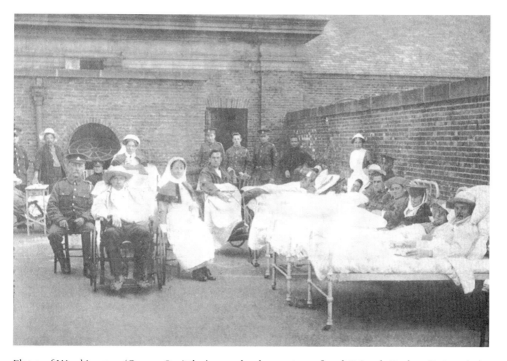

Flat-roof Ward in 1917. (George Sprittles's scrapbook, courtesy of and © Leeds Beckett University)

Ambulances at the ready in 1917. (George Sprittles's scrapbook, courtesy of and © Leeds Beckett University)

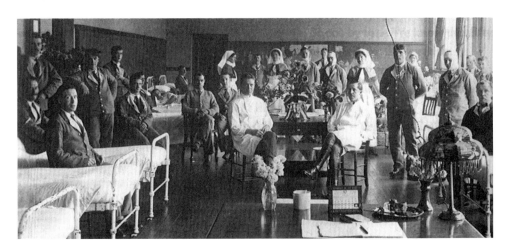

The Jaw Ward in 1916. (George Sprittles's scrapbook, courtesy of and © Leeds Beckett University)

plays and billiards. In March 1916 temporary huts were erected for a 700-bed annexe. However, it was apparently not all patient care and recuperation. James Graham, Director of Education for Leeds, was appalled by women students 'disporting themselves in unseemly ways' while soldiers were often to be seen thronging the tennis courts to watch the women playing.

Maxillofacial workshop at the hospital, 1916. (George Sprittles's scrapbook, courtesy of and © Leeds Beckett University)

The Cheerio Boys providing entertainment in 1918. (George Sprittles's scrapbook, courtesy of and © Leeds Beckett University)

Auxiliary Military Hospital, Temple Newsam
In October 1914 Lady Dorothy Wood gave over the south wing of Temple Newsam for the nursing of fifty recovering disabled soldiers, mainly officers. Initially it was intended to receive wounded Belgian officers, sixteen of them after the fall of Antwerp. When it closed three years later, 615 patients had been nursed by Lady Wood, her two professional nurses and seven VAD nurses and household staff.

Chapel Allerton Military Hospital
Chapel Allerton opened in March 1916 with thirty-five beds; when it closed in April 1919 it could boast fifty-seven beds with a total of 1,320 wounded soldiers having benefited from its care.

Convalescence hospitals
After treatment in these hospitals as above, patients would be transferred to one of twenty or so Leeds auxiliary hospitals for convalescence. Many of these were in local country houses, loaned by their owners. They included Gledhow Hall, Harewood House,

Recovering soldiers in Killingbeck Municipal Sanatorium; the hospital was built in 1913 on the Killingbeck Hall estate.

Lotherton Hall, Stapleton Park, Ledstone Hall, Swillington House and hospitals based in Chapeltown and Roundhay. Museums and art galleries did their bit too in accommodating the recuperating.

Gledhow Hall Auxiliary Hospital opened in 1915 as a fifty-bed VAD hospital, it was run by Edith Cliff, cousin of Lord Airedale, the owner. Its role was to take referrals from Beckett's Park. Twelve VADs did the nursing and even formed their own cricket team. There was also croquet, bowling, golf and skating on the lake in winter to aid recovery.

Lotherton Hall opened in November 1914; the owner, Colonel Gascoigne refused to accept the government grant he was entitled to and funded the hospital himself. He converted his motor car into an ambulance and toured the Western Front tending the wounded. Magnanimously, the colonel insisted on treating only other ranks and no officers at Lotherton Hall. Recreation included shooting parties. Lotherton opened with eighteen beds but expanded to thirty-five soon after the start of the Somme offensive.

Armley House

This was Leeds's tuberculosis hospital, TB being a notifiable disease after 1912. It was a convalescent hospital with forty-four beds.

Recuperation, of course, can be dull and drawn out at the best of times – particularly for men with recent experience of battle despite the stresses it brought. In a bid to allay the monotony H. Clifford Bowling, a local cartoonist, set up the Leeds War Hospital Entertainment Scheme as a registered charity in 1916. This involved two shows every week at Beckett's Park and more at Killingbeck, including concerts, theatrical performances, films, talks by enthusiasts and performances by patients. Local voluntary organizations arranged outings for convalescents and occasional sports days.

Hospital journals sprang up, edited by hospital staff, and sold to raise funds. Patients were encouraged to contribute stories, art work and poetry. The journal of No. 2 Northern General at Beckett's Park was *The Blue Band*. Editions from 1919 include articles on pensions for veterans, cinema news, 'The Day in a Military Hospital' and 'The Wiring Party', a spoof on men out of their beds after lights out.

Charles F. Thackray surgical suppliers

Thackray's grew rapidly from a small retail pharmacy to a global surgical supply company employing 700 people and selling pharmaceuticals, medical instruments and surgical equipment; they pioneered the hip replacement operation we know today as a positive boon to hundreds of thousands of people. Thackray's premises were on the corner of Great George Street and Portland Street, near the infirmary. It is hardly surprising that the war saw a steep increase in the demand for dressings which in those days were sewn onto bandages by hand. To meet this demand Thackray's invested in a machine to make the 'Washington Haigh Field Dressing' both economically and speedily. Thackray's aseptic range won War Office approval as the standard field dressing and led to additional business contracts across the company's range of products.

British War Graves Association

Everybody is familiar with the superb work done by the Imperial War Graves Commission, later the Commonwealth War Graves Commission. Fewer, though, know much about the British War Graves Association, founded in Leeds in 1919. The founder was Sarah Ann Smith, who lived in Stourton; she lost her son, Frederick Ernest, who died of wounds in 1918 and lies buried at Grevellers near Arras. Sarah Smith firmly believed that soldiers killed in action who could be brought home for burial should be. This conviction was encapsulated in a letter, probably by Mrs Smith:

> Now the government has decided to remove the bodies of the fallen from the scattered cemeteries to large central cemeteries, why cannot they allow relatives who so desire to have them brought home to be placed in the family grave?
>
> Nurse Cavell's body is being brought over to England, and why not others?
>
> I think the feeling is very strong against this attitude of the government, who claimed our boys when living, and now they have sacrificed their lives we are to be robbed of their dear remains, which belong to us and are ours alone.

A further letter outlined the action to be taken:

> In view of the decision of the Government to remove the remains of the fallen from the scattered cemeteries in France and Belgium to new cemeteries, a petition is being got up to the Prince of Wales, as President of The War Graves Commission, to allow those relations who so wish, to have the bodies brought over to this country. Anyone having suffered loss are invited to give their names to the petition.

Three years later we learn from the *Rothwell Courier & Times* on 13 May 1922 that the petition 'was unsuccessful, but a large proportion of the two thousand five hundred signatories formed the nucleus of the [The British War Graves Association] which has now its central branch in Leeds, and branches in Sheffield and Wakefield'. After much debate, letters to the press and many meetings, on 18 June 1921 the *Rothwell Courier* published another letter on the topic on its front page, sent by the Countess of Selborne to Mrs Smith:

> There is one aspect of compulsory burying all the gallant men who fell in defence of France in that country, to which I think sufficient attention has not been given.
>
> A very large sum has been spent in beautifying these cemeteries, and certainly no one would wish to stint money in honouring our glorious dead, but how little security we have that the monuments erected at so much expense will be maintained, and how few of their fellow countrymen will see them.
>
> Many things may happen which would cause their destruction. In future times there may be wars there in which we will not take part [and] the great stones may serve either side for gun emplacements. There may be riots.
>
> For some reason or other England may be unpopular in France at that moment, and the cemeteries might be wrecked by the mob.
>
> How much better it would have been to have had the State cemeteries – if State cemeteries are desired – on the British coast where they could have always been admired and cherished by our own people, and those who wished to have their own dead buried near their homes, might have been gratified at little extra expense.
> Yours truly,
> Maud Selborne

The efforts of the British War Graves Association to bring home the dead came to nothing. And we now know that the fears of the Countess of Selborne likewise came to nothing. The British War Graves Association did however organize and assist many people to visit the graves of their fallen at Whitsun every year. Mrs Smith missed only one year before her death in 1936.

Hyde Park Picture House

The 1914 opening was promoted by an advertisement in the *Yorkshire Evening Post* which, amid all the war news, heralded the new picture house as 'The Cosiest in Leeds'. Apart from patriotic films, the picture house also showed newsreels of the war to the people of Leeds, anxious to learn about the 6,000 men from Leeds who had enlisted, and reliant on the picture house news because many of them could not read the newspapers or afford a wireless. The Empire and Hippodrome also showed war news and at the Empire the audiences stood up at the end to the French and Russian national anthems in addition to usual 'God Save the King' and 'Rule Britannia'.

Industry and Commerce

Barnbow Munitions Factory – National Filling Factory No. 1

Barnbow was a First World War munitions factory located between Cross Gates and Garforth, officially known as National Filling Factory No. 1. Sadly, Barnbow is best known for the massive explosion which killed thirty-five women workers in 1916.

When war was declared, shells were being filled and armed at Leeds Forge Company, Armley, which by August 1915 was filling 10,000 shells every week. This, however, was insufficient to meet demand so the newly formed Leeds Munitions Committee promoted production of shells at Hunslet and Newlay (Horsforth). The committee comprised six Leeds citizens and was charged with the construction of the First National Shell Filling Factory. They met in August 1915 and a site was selected at Barnbow, part of the Gascoigne estate. A committee, chaired by Joseph Watson, the Leeds soap manufacturer, was set up to build the new munitions factory.

Railway tracks were laid, running into the factory complex to carry materials in and finished goods out. There were thirteen miles of wide-gauge railway track and ten miles of narrow trolley track. Platforms over 800 feet long were added to the nearby railway station to help transport workers to and from work at the site; the Yorkshire Power Company erected a 10kv overhead line to a sub-station and this, in conjunction with a boiler house and heating plant, provided power for the heating and lighting of the entire complex. The electric power cables extended for over twenty-eight miles. A water main was laid to deliver 200,000 gallons of water per day and a 90,000-gallon collecting and screening tank was built to collect waste, which was pumped to the Leeds Sewerage Works at Killingbeck. The service mains – water, sewage, and fire – extended for thirty-three miles, and the steam and hot-water piping for sixty miles. Coal was supplied by rail from Garforth Collieries Ltd. and Wheldale Coal Co. In April 1916, the first batch of thirty 4½-inch shells

Barnbow girls making box lids for cartridge packing cases out of empty propellant boxes. They are using circular saws (without protective guards) to cut the wood to size to make the box lids. (Courtesy of Leodis © Leeds Library & Information Services)

were filled, the output quickly increasing to 6,000 shells a day, when the number of shifts was increased from two to three.

Recruitment took place at an employment bureau at Wellesley Barracks, Leeds; the first batch of employees was sent to Woolwich for one month's training after which training was all done at Barnbow. Around 130,000 female applicants were interviewed. One third of the staff was from Leeds while others commuted from York, Castleford, Selby, Tadcaster, Wetherby, Knaresborough, Wakefield and Harrogate; by October 1916 the workforce exceeded 16,000 people, 93 per cent of which was women and girls – 'The Barnbow Lasses'. Thirty-eight trains per day, 'Barnbow Specials', carried the workers to and from work.

The women worked a system of three eight-hour shifts: 6 a.m. to 2 p.m., 2 p.m. to 10 p.m. and 10 p.m. to 6 a.m. usually on a six-days-a-week rota, with Saturday off every

Barnbow girls, women and men.

three weeks; there were no holidays. A typical munition worker's earnings for a full week averaged £3; the girls who swept up the waste for recycling earned £1/17- a week. Extra money was paid to workers in the dangerous powder room. At one point the weekly wage bill totalled £24,000.

Ancillary services included canteens, nurse stations, administration and changing rooms. There were qualified nurses and an in-house doctor, two dentists with a fully equipped surgery to care for the workers. Fire was obviously a constant hazard, monitored by a fire brigade which had access to a 300,000-gallon reservoir to supplement the link to the city's water supply. Men of the Royal Defence Corps guarded the factory.

The catering facilities were most impressive. There were three canteens, the largest seating 4,000 workers at two sittings of forty-five minutes. The kitchens were state of the art including electric cookers, potato peelers, mincing machines, large pudding and potato steamers, and vegetable boilers. A hot drinks buffet was available for use by staff who brought in their own food. In 1916 farm buildings were adapted to house 120 cows, tended by six girls, under the supervision of a qualified farm bailiff; the dairy produced 300 gallons of milk every day; Barnbow had its own slaughterhouse, butcher's shop and bacon factory that supplied fresh meat. Land was cultivated for crops and in 1918 some 200 tons of potatoes were grown.

Logistics were impressive too. A two-foot-gauge track transported small loads around the factory, power courtesy of seventy ponies. Heavier loads were shifted by trains hauling 150 trucks a day in 1916 to over 600 trucks a day in 1918 behind eight locomotives. At the end of the war 10,000 tons a week of munitions were moved; total monthly tonnage of materials shifted in and out of the factory was around 100,000 tons. There were two receiving stores: one at Royds Green in Rothwell, the other at Woodlesford; Army Service Corps did the driving and provided the vehicles. The factory boasted a fully equipped garage to service and maintain the passenger cars and ambulances which were driven by women chauffeurs of the Women's Legion.

The local textile industry was heavily involved in supplying huge quantities of material for nearly 87 million cartridge bags and 26 million exploder bags and smoke bags – all these and smaller components were manufactured in Leeds. Leeds textile stores not only supplied Barnbow but all the filling factories in the country. There were six acres of floor space used in the four warehouses near Wellington Street. Here, staff dealt with over 27 million yards of textile materials in the piece, nearly 142 million yards of braids and tapes, 150 tons of sewing threads and 9,354 tons of millboard and strawboard. This industry also fed into the local printing trade, leading to the invention of a new system of printing on the bags.

Demand for munitions was seemingly inexhaustible: in 1917 the site was extended to increase storage for finished ammunition when fourteen large magazines were built on Crossgates golf course. The chemical engineering involved was as follows: 12,000 tons of trinitrotoluene (TNT) was mixed with 26,350 tons of ammonium nitrate to produce the highly explosive Amatol compound. In the cartridge factory 61,000 tons of propellant was made into breech-loading charges made up of NCT and cordite.

Some aspects of health and safety were encouragingly advanced. Sandbags and protective shields were all around the place; sprinklers and drenchers were attached to the magazines; there were fireproof doors and protective earthworks. There was good ventilation in the work areas, especially in the Amatol factories; initially staff were limited to a fortnight stretch anywhere where TNT was handled. All workers had to pass a medical examination before starting their employment; those working in dangerous area zones had a periodic medical examination. A female superintendent, supported by a staff of welfare workers, was appointed to make regular visits to employees, either during work or at meal times. They also visited anyone off sick or absent from work for any length of time. Tennis courts were provided. The fire brigade was an early introduction: initially it was all men but later, girls were trained up. Eventually thirty girls and six firemen, under the command of an experienced London firemaster from London, made up the brigade.

Units of the Royal Defence Corps provided security, maintaining a twenty-four-hour patrol of the security fence and gates. The superintendent of police with three inspectors

Fire practice at Barnbow.

controlled the male police, while a female superintendent was in charge of policewomen for female search purposes. All personnel were required to wear identity discs and to carry permits; there were frequent body and bag searches. Dangerous areas were under constant surveillance, with 'safe' areas reserved for smokers. There was a complete press blackout of the area.

Despite this the work was still very dangerous. Workers who handled the explosives stripped to their underwear, and wore smocks, puttees, caps, rubber gloves and rubber-soled boots to avoid sparks; cigarettes and matches were obviously banned as were combs and hairpins to prevent static electricity. Workers were allowed to drink as much barley water and milk as they liked. Working with cordite turned the skin yellow: the only known antidote was milk. Because of the yellowness of the women's skin, they were called 'The Barnbow Canaries'.

On Tuesday 5 December 1916, 170 women and girls had just started their night shift in one of the fusing rooms: 4½-inch shells were being filled, fused, and packed in Room 42. At 10.27 p.m. there was a massive explosion which killed thirty-five women outright, and maimed and injured many more. Many of the dead were only identifiable by their identity disks. The injured were taken to the Leeds General Infirmary with the help of the factory medical staff, the ambulance corps and the voluntary motor transport section. Production was interrupted only for a short time, and once the bodies were recovered, other girls immediately volunteered to replace them in Room 42.

For reasons of security, none of this was made public until 1924; at the time death notices appeared in the *Yorkshire Evening Post*, simply stating cause of death as 'killed by accident' and other euphemisms. There were two further explosions at the factory; the first in March 1917 killing two girls, the other in May 1918 killing three men.

Barnbow was Britain's premier shell factory between 1914 and 1918. By 11 November 1918, a total of 566,000 tons of ammunition had been shipped to the various fronts; over 36 million breech-loading cartridges had been produced; 24.75 million shells had been filled; and a further 19.25 million shells had been fused and packed: a grand total of 566,000 tons of finished ammunition exported. Of 18-pounder shells 9¼ million were filled which, if laid end to end, covered a distance of 3,200 miles.

Apart from setting up the dignified memorial, in 2012 the people of Leeds named a number of parks, buildings and streets in memory of the 'Barnbow Lasses'. The names of those who died are listed in the roll of honour in Colton Methodist church, and in York Minster near the Five Sisters Window. Louise Birch, from Local and Family History, Leeds Central Library has researched some very tragic and moving details about the casualties, as given in her 'Remembering the Barnbow Tragedy: 100 Years Ago Today' (https://secretlibraryleeds. net/tag/barnbow/). Here are just a few of the thirty-seven, selected at random:

Amelia Stewart of Leeds, aged 28: died twenty-five days later in hospital from internal injuries, 30 December 1916. (Today, Amelia Stewart Lane on the old Barnbow site is named in her honour.)

Kate Bainbridge of Leeds was 40 years old at the time of her death. Kate was married with four children. Her husband William served with the West Yorkshire Regiment, but had become ill with pulmonary tuberculosis and spent most of 1916 in hospital. On 6 December 1916 his doctor recommended permanent discharge with the following report: 'Not a result but aggravated by active service exposure. Permanent is getting worse. Total incapacity. Very hard case. Wife killed last night in Barnbow explosion, and he has 4 children, eldest 9. He is extremely ill and urgently needs money. Earnings – nil.' William Bainbridge died 27 February 1918.

Edith Sykes of Leeds, died aged 15: Edith's older sister Agnes also worked in Barnbow's Room 42 but on the night of the explosion Agnes was home sick with flu. Edith was injured in the explosion and taken to Leeds Infirmary where she died several weeks later. Her older brother Herbert was in the army, based in York and borrowed a gun carriage from his barracks to carry Edith's coffin. It is probable that Edith lied about her age to work at Barnbow.

Emily Sedgwick of Harrogate, died aged 39: Emily was not injured in the Barnbow explosion but died two years later. The coroner found her condition to be related to the shock she suffered in the 1916 incident.

Mary E. Carter of York, died aged 22: *Yorkshire Herald*, 16 December 1916: 'Women patriot's funeral at York of soldier's young wife … The funeral took place at York cemetery yesterday of Mary Elizabeth Carter, aged 22, daughter of Mr and Mrs Eshelby, 3, Fettergate-lane, Micklegate, York, and wife of Lance-Corporal W. Carter, who met her death last week under tragic circumstances. There is one child, aged two years. A brother is serving in France … She was formerly employed at Messrs. Rowntree's factory. There were pathetic scenes at the funeral, which was largely attended, a number of the deceased's fellow-workers heading the cortege.'

Olive Yeates of York: Olive was survived by three children and a husband with tuberculosis. Rumours handed down by survivors reported that Olive was working on the shell that exploded. Today, Olive Yeates Way on the old Barnbow site is named in her honour.

The Five Sisters Memorial in York Minster honouring local munitions workers who died in service, including Barnbow girls and women. This is the only memorial in the country to the women of the British Empire who lost their lives during the First World War. The names of the 1,400 women commemorated are inscribed on oak screens on the north side of the St Nicholas's Chapel. This memorial lists by far the greatest number of names of any in the minster or cathedral, including that of Edith Cavell, the British nurse shot by a German firing squad in 1915.

Eliza Grant of Castleford, died aged 39: she left seven children aged between 6 and 17, all now considered as in 'partial dependency of her income of 19s 6d'. They were granted £65 compensation from the Ministry of Munitions. A story passed down from Eliza's descendants says that 5 December was Eliza's day off; however, as she had completed all her housework before the last bus left for the factory she decided to go in on the advice of a friend. Eliza was killed as she arrived, walking through the door of Room 42 as the shell exploded.

Royal Ordnance Factory, Newlay

Leeds had three other shell factories: one was the Royal Ordnance Factory at Newlay which opened in 1916 down Hunters Greave in Bramley, covering five acres. In the beginning it was staffed just by men; later, thirty women were taken on then several hundred. At its height the total workforce exceeded 1,000. As noted, there was a third shell factory, in Armley in the former Leeds Forge Company, and a fourth at Hunslet.

Some employers were keen to see their men enlist, promising that their jobs would be held open for them on their return. Hepworths even contributed £2 towards kit and gave 5s a week to dependents while staff were away. Less philanthropic were Chadwick Brothers, textile manufacturers of Hunslet, who threatened with dismissal any worker aged between 18 and 35 who had not tried to enlist by 4 September. However, those who did enlist did so with a promise of their job back on return and 10s per week for dependents while they were serving. Leeds Corporation was particularly generous, and persuasive: jobs were secure, and

Shells being assembled at Newlay.

for non-manual workers, half their salary was paid while away. Manual workers got 5s per week for dependents while the wives of married men received 5s per week plus 2s per week extra for every child under fifteen. By August 1914 the Corporation had paid out £34,484.

Joshua Tetley & Sons

The records of the Leeds Rifles, *Quartermaster Sergeant's Chest (1859–1938)*, list the officers of the company, as well as the regimental regulations. In 'A Century's Progress' it records the number of Tetley employees who served in 1914: 'Out of the six hundred and thirteen employees of Tetley's in 1914, no less than two hundred and sixty-one served in the army, mostly (242) on the battle fronts in various parts of the world. Twenty-five of these fine soldiers paid the price of life itself.'

The war was, of course, commercially disruptive. Out of its 613-strong workforce, 261 (43 per cent) left for war. A memorial to the Tetley fallen was unveiled on 17 November 1922, created by the employees and displayed in the entrance hall leading to the brewery's offices.

The introduction of conscription boosted the surge of women recruited by Tetley's. Most were employed in the maltings and the offices, while some were given jobs in the mash room or worked as painters. While they soon showed they could do the jobs just as well as the men had done, it did not mean they were paid the same wage. Women received 25 or 27 shillings a week, compared with 33 shillings for most men. As the war went on the company's profits grew, as did the workers' wages, although again it was the men who benefited most. By the end of the war the disparity was even greater.

Tetley's not only contributed men to the Leeds Rifles. Before the First World War they provided horses and men for a battery of the rapid reaction, highly mobile Leeds Artillery with their four 4.7-inch guns. Horses were also sent to field ambulance units of the Royal Army Medical Corps. In 1984 the Leeds Rifle Company of the 1st Battalion Yorkshire Volunteers at Carlton New Barracks adopted two shire horses as mascots, Mild and Bitter, to mark the raising of Tetley's No. 9 Company 125 years before.

Burton's

Burton's was founded by Montague Burton in Chesterfield in 1904 under the name of the Cross-Tailoring Company. Burton himself was a Russian-Jewish immigrant, origi-nally Meshe David Osinsky. He arrived in England from Russia aged 15 working as a peddler, and three years later borrowed £100 from a relative to open the Cross-Tailoring Company. Records show that the first purchase of readymade suits was on 8 June 1905, from Zimmerman Bros., wholesale clothiers of Leeds. The growing business moved to Elmwood Mills, Camp Road in Leeds, but by 1914 it had outgrown these premises and transferred to Concord Mills, Concord Street.

By 1914 the number of Burton shops increased to fourteen and their made-to-measure service was well on the way to becoming the largest in the world. The First World War

Busy Burton's staff at the factory in Hudson Road, Harehills.

saw Burton's become an official war contractor and production switched from suits to uniforms, clothing nearly 25 per cent of the armed forces. Retail sales grew from £52,000 in 1915 to £150,000 in 1917 with a further £60,000 outstanding. In 1918 demob suits and bespoke suits were very much in demand.

Joseph Hepworth & Son, also of Leeds and now Next plc, became the largest clothing manufacturer in the UK during the war.

Northern Area Army Clothing Depot

The Army Clothing Depot opened in Swinegate, Leeds, near what was then the Midland Railway station, in King's Mills next to what was originally the Tramways Depot. The War Office requisitioned and adapted it for the 'handling of pieces of khaki cloth and uniforms'. By May 1915 more storage space was needed so the cattle market buildings in Gelderd Road were taken over to store cloth – up to 9 million yards of it. Three million uniforms were also stored in another depot, belonging to the Aire & Calder Navigation. A Park Row premises saw 80,000 shirts inspected every week. All told, The Northern Area produced 53 million shirts, 21 million pairs of army trousers, 8 million pairs of cavalry trousers, 10 million greatcoats, 24 million puttees, 89 million pairs of socks and 30 million

Workers checking in bales of cloth from Newcastle, Staffordshire.

pairs of boots. Apart from production and inspection, the depots also recycled uniforms and other clothing salvaged from battlefield casualties.

Before the Leeds depot opened the system for uniform manufacture and provision was cumbersome to say the least. Hitherto, cloth produced in northern mills was sent, by rail, to the Central Army Clothing Depot in Pimlico, London where it was checked and tested, and sent back to Yorkshire for making up.

The new Leeds depot with its 150 staff revolutionized the process and answered the endless need for more and more uniforms; it enabled cloth to be processed locally in a timely fashion. By the end of the war some 750,000 uniforms per week were passing through Leeds, some of which was produced by Edwin Woodhouse & Co. Ltd. in Farsley.

In 1918, according to the *Illustrated London News* (Issue 4129 Vol CLII 8 June 1918), the authorities ordered 95 million yards of cloth, 5 million yards of flannel, over 82 million items of hosiery, and 16 million blankets for processing through factories in Leeds, Shipley, Saltaire, and Keighley, Dewsbury, Batley, Heckmondwike and Huddersfield. In total the War Office bought 600 million pounds of British and Colonial wool, costing £104 million.

Zeppelins

Leeds was never bombed by a Zeppelin but, naturally, precautions were put in place in and around the city. Special constables were tasked with keeping watch, mainly from the roof of the Town Hall, and with raising the alarm. Spotting a Zeppelin would trigger a reduction in gas and electricity supply, a dimming of all lights and stopping the trams. The only two raids to speak of were in September and November 1916 when Zeppelins passed over Collingham and Pontefract Park: incendiaries were dropped on the grounds of Harewood House when the Germans perhaps confused the Aire with the Wharfe. The *Daily News* offered free insurance against Zeppelin damage!

Military engineering

Hunslet Locomotive Works was where 4-6-0 locomotives were built to run on the supply lines on the Western Front. Kirkstall Forge turned out axles. After 1916 Sopwith Camels were built in Leeds – seventy-five by March, Jones & Cribb in York Road. All told, Sopwith Camel pilots downed 1,294 German aircraft. They saw service with the Royal Flying Corps, the Royal Naval Air Service and the United States Air Service. More aircraft were constructed at the Blackburn Company's Roundhay Road Britannia Works.

Chemical research

The British aniline dye industry was seriously impaired by the outbreak of war; by February 1915 there remained a mere three months' supply of dyes left in the United Kingdom. Aniline dyes were essential in both civilian and military clothing production. To make matters even worse, coal tar, from which aniline dyes are derived, was hijacked for use in the manufacture of the explosive tri-nitrotoluene (TNT). Professor Arthur Green was Chair of Tinctorial (Colour) Chemistry at the University of Leeds from 1903 to 1916 and one of the chemists in a committee tasked with solving the problems of chemical supplies required for dyes and explosives. The committee established British Dyes Ltd. to alleviate the aniline dye shortage. Green then focused on increasing explosives production, developing a better way of making picric acid, a key component in explosives, also useful as an antiseptic and for burns treatment. Green's sterling work at Leeds was continued by Arthur Perkin.

Professor of Chemistry Arthur Smithells' main contribution was instructing troops in gas warfare: he served as a visiting lecturer to the camps of the Northern Command and later as chief chemical adviser for anti-gas training of the Home Forces, attaining the honorary rank of lieutenant-colonel. Smithells proceeded to demystify the science underpinning gas warfare by educating the troops in effective responses to its use, banishing what he termed the scientific and chemical 'illiteracy', and promulgating an understanding of the basic chemical principles involved. Smithell debunked many of the myths surrounding war gas, not least the instinctive reaction of the soldier to flee or seek refuge at the bottom of a trench, whereas in reality it was those who stayed at their posts rather than those who ran away, and those who remained on the fire step rather than at the bottom of the trench where the gas was at is densest, who suffered least.

Agriculture

War obviously brings a damaging reduction in imported goods and agricultural workers vanished from the fields and farms as they signed up for active service. The University of Leeds undertook valuable research to minimize the debilitating effects of war on food supply and land use, not least in the growth of flax, the training of women and ex-servicemen who volunteered for farm work, and the support given to local allotments and training centres throughout Yorkshire.

Flax was a vital material in the manufacture of the aeroplane, emerging as a crucial weapon of war. Fibres from the flax plant were used to make linen which was stretched and treated with chemicals to construct the wings of fighter aircraft. It was imported from Belgium and Russia before the war so the British government was now forced to expand domestic production. The Flax Experiment Station had already been established at Selby in 1913 under the auspices of the University of Leeds and military demand for flax led to the work carried out at Selby grow more than twentyfold between 1914 and 1918; acreage increased from 120 to 2,600 acres, extending to North Lincolnshire by the end of the war.

Training women for farm work was important too, in order to replace the depleted male work force. Courses for women were held at the university's experimental farm at Garforth, one of twelve training centres established across the country for this purpose.

Anti-Semitism

The night of 3/4 June 1917 saw the outbreak of ugly scenes of anti-Jewish violence in the Jewish quarter of Leeds: Bridge Street, North Street and Regent Street. Street fighting led to the vandalism and looting of Jewish premises and businesses while Jewish soldiers were attacked. The police were accused of complacency. It had obviously escaped the notice of the perpetrators that of the 25,000 or so Jews in Leeds at the time, 2,500 had enlisted for military service, and that despite the exemptions for those engaged in war work such as tailoring.

The university also supported work-based training courses in which about a hundred ex-servicemen were seconded to farmers to complete a two-year programme of farm training. Course material was created by the university's Department of Agriculture.

The Richmond Sixteen

High casualty rates and falling numbers of recruits meant that by 1916 military conscription was introduced. Under the conscription laws men could apply for exemption from military service on the grounds of ill health, hardship, occupation or conscientious objection. Thousands did, although only a small number did so on the grounds of conscience; few, however, were granted total exemption from war service and were ordered to join the Non-Combatant Corps (NCC). 27,000 applicants went before the Leeds Tribunal in over 55,000 hearings at 435 sittings between 1916 and 1918. Most were withdrawn or dismissed, sending the applicants to the services or the NCC. The case of the claimant who appealed against his enlistment so that he could compete a three-month hair-treatment course was not typical.

Richmond Castle became a base for the NCC, and thousands of conscientious objectors (COs) were sent there. Among them were the Richmond Sixteen, a group of 'absolutist' British conscientious objectors who refused to undertake even non-combatant military duties. They were shipped to France where one recanted and the other

COs at Dyce.

fifteen were court-martialled and sentenced to be executed by firing squad; this was commuted to ten years' penal servitude. On 11 July 1917 Alfred Martlew was found drowned in the River Ouse at York; the remaining fourteen were released in 1919. Back home they were disfranchised for five years and ostracized by their communities and employers.

The Richmond Sixteen are remembered for the mass of graffiti they left in their gaol. The Richmond Sixteen included Methodists, a Congregationalist, a Quaker, International Bible Students (Jehovah's Witnesses), a lay reader and socialists; eight were from Leeds:

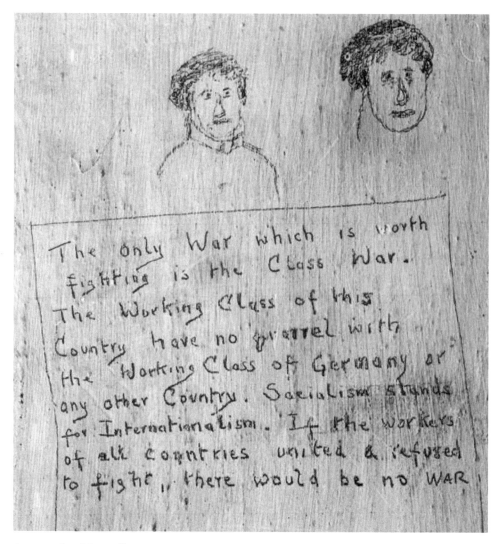

An example of the graffiti.

Leonard Renton, a draughtsman

Charles Rowland Jackson, a clerk at a Leeds wool merchant

Clifford Cartwright, a printer

Charles Herbert Senior, a carpenter and cabinet maker

Ernest Shillito Spencer, a clerk in a Leeds clothing factory

The Hall brothers – Clarence, a joiner's clerk, and Stafford, a draughtsman for Leeds
    Corporation sewage works

John William Routledge, a clerk at the Leeds steel works.

The Beeston Brotherhood

The Beeston Brotherhood was a Tolstoyan group of anarchist pacifists and vegetarians who came to settle in Leeds from Surrey in 1904. They were investigated under DORA, the Defence of the Realm Act, while their literature was deemed prejudicial to recruitment, training and discipline. The anarchist, Alf Kitson, was a prominent member, described as a joiner when he appeared in Hull Police Court charged with refusing to fill up a registration under the Registration Act, on 21 February 1916. He asserted that 'I refuse to give you any information. I do not believe in slaying my fellow men, and I will not have part or lot in the making of munitions of war. I have no more faith in you than I have in the Kaiser. You all believe in murder and robbery, and you will not give justice to the workers of our land in times of peace. You make the wars, so fight them yourselves. I have had nothing to do with the foreign policy, never having voted for representatives in Parliament. You may do what you like, but I refuse to assist you.'

He had already been summonsed under the same charge on 4 February, but had failed to appear and was arrested. The magistrate urged Kitson to change his mind, but he persisted and was heavily fined.

The Leeds founder, Tom Ferris, with accomplice Overbury, was jailed in Armley where they went on hunger strike. Overbury was force-fed but the medical authorities refused to sanction this due to his 'weak heart'. More arrests followed at known Brotherhood addresses which became refuges for conscientious objectors.

The Leeds Convention

The eight Leeds men of the Richmond Sixteen and the Beeston Brotherhood were not the only Leeds men opposed to fighting in the war. Soon after the Russian Revolution in 1917 a mass Labour and Socialist convention was held in support of the revolution at Leeds Coliseum. Some 3,500 democrats and socialists, including nearly 300 from the Independent Labour Party, pledged solidarity with the Russian Revolution and voted to set up workers' and soldiers' councils in Britain.

It did not go down well locally. When the delegates arrived their hotel bookings had been cancelled by the hotel proprietors. The temperance hotels were the 'worst offenders'.

Alternative accommodation was found but late arrivals were forced to spend the night in railway carriages. The booking of the Albert Hall in the Mechanics' Institute, where the meeting was to have been held, was cancelled, and the delegates diverted to the Coliseum in Cookridge Street. The council and police also banned an open-air assembly arranged for Victoria Square. A subsequent meeting to be held in Leeds was cancelled by the government.

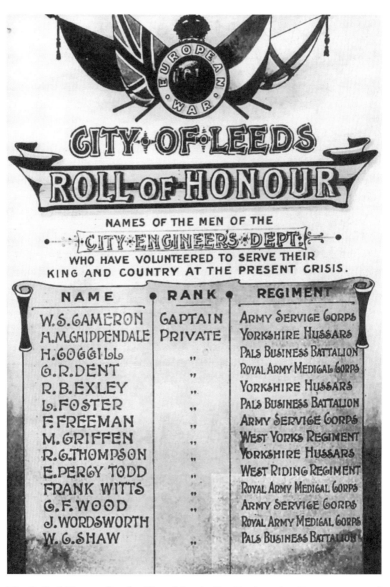

The Roll of Honour for the City of Leeds City Engineering Department and their regiments. (© Martin Edwards 2006, www.roll-of-honour.com)

Rolls of Honour

Headingley Rugby Football Club sent 190 men to join the various forces: forty-seven died while twenty-two were decorated. The Yarnbury Club had fourteen die out of the fifty who signed up; four members were decorated. Thirty-eight boys from Leeds Grammar School enlisted of whom seven were killed and two decorated. Leeds Grammar School paid a particularly heavy price. There are 130 names on the First World War roll (and 109 on the Second World War roll). 777 former pupils took part in First World War.

For the full list see www.gsal.org.uk/alumni/gsal-roll-of-honour/

Leeds's Victoria Crosses

Captain David Philip Hirsch

Hirsch was born on 28 December 1896 to Harry and Edith Hirsch of Weetwood Grove, Leeds. He was 20 years old at the time of his brave action, and an acting captain in the 4th Battalion, The Yorkshire Regiment (Alexandra, Princess of Wales's Own). On 23 April 1917 near Wancourt, France, he performed a deed for which he was awarded the Victoria Cross. He died in action that day. Having arrived at the first objective, Captain Hirsch, although already twice wounded, returned over fire-swept slopes to satisfy himself that the defensive flank was being established. Machine-gun fire was so intense that it was necessary for him to be continuously up and down the line encouraging his men to dig and hold the position. He continued to encourage his men by standing on the parapet and steadying them in the face of machine-gun fire and counterattack until he was killed.

Captain George Sanders

George Sanders, from Holbeck, was awarded both the VC and the MC. He was educated at Little Holbeck School and became an apprentice fitter at the Airedale Foundry.

For the Victoria Cross: for most conspicuous bravery (near Thiepval, France). After an advance into the enemy's trenches, he found himself isolated with a party of thirty men. He organized his defences, detailed a bombing party, and impressed on his men that his and their duty was to hold the position at all costs. Next morning he drove off an attack by the enemy and rescued some prisoners who had fallen into their hands. Later two strong bombing attacks were beaten off. On the following day he was relieved after showing the greatest courage, determination and good leadership during thirty-six hours under very trying conditions. All this time his party was without food and water, having given all their water to the wounded during the first night. After the relieving force was firmly established, he brought his party, nineteen strong, back to our trenches.

For the award of the Military Cross: for conspicuous gallantry and devotion to duty. After the enemy had penetrated the front line, he promptly organized his men in support and effectually held up the enemy for some time, inflicting heavy casualties. He stood on top of a pill-box firing his revolver into the enemy of twenty yards. His splendid example of courage did much to inspire his men at a critical time.

Following George Sanders's Military Cross action he was taken prisoner and sent to the Limburg prisoner of war camp, repatriated to England on 26 December 1918. On 1 March 2017 his VC and MC were sold on auction for £240,000.

Private William Boynton Butler

Private Butler was from Hunslet. For the award of the Victoria Cross: for most conspicuous bravery (east of Lempire, France) when in charge of a Stokes gun [a 3-inch trench mortar invented by Sir Wilfred Stokes] in trenches which were being heavily shelled. Suddenly one of the fly-off levers of a Stokes shell came off and fired the shell in the emplacement. Private Butler picked up the shell and jumped to the entrance of the emplacement, which at that moment a party of infantry were passing. He shouted to them to hurry past as the shell was going off, and turning round, placed himself between the party of men and the live shell and so held it till they were out of danger. He then threw the shell on to the parados, and took cover in the bottom the trench. The shell exploded almost on leaving his hand, greatly damaging the trench. By extreme good luck Private Butler was contused only. Undoubtedly his great presence of mind and disregard of his own life saved the lives of the officer and men in the emplacement and the party which was passing at the time. Butler was also awarded the Croix de Guerre.

Sergeant Albert Mountain

Albert Mountain, from Garforth, was awarded his VC while serving as a sergeant in the 15/17th Battalion, The Prince of Wales's Own (West Yorkshire Regiment) – Leeds Pals. On 21 March 1918 at Hamelincourt, France, when the situation was critical, Sergeant Mountain with a party of ten men attacked an advance enemy patrol of about 200 strong with a Lewis gun, killing half of them. The sergeant then rallied his men in the face of overwhelming numbers of the main body of the enemy, to cover the retirement of the rest of the company – this party of one NCO and four men held at bay 600 of the enemy for half an hour. Sergeant Mountain later took command of the flank post of the battalion, holding on for twenty-seven hours until finally surrounded. He was also awarded the Croix de Guerre and Médaille Militaire. Albert Mountain was landlord of the Miners' Arms in Garforth for twenty-five years.

Private Arthur Poulter

Arthur Poulter was born in 1893 East Witton and lived in New Wortley. Before the war he was employed as a drayman at the Timothy Taylor Brewery, Leeds. At the time of the action for which he was awarded the VC, he was 24 years old, and a private in the 1/4th Battalion, The Duke of Wellington's (West Riding) Regiment. On 10 April 1918 at Erquinghem-Lys, France, Private Poulter, who was acting as a stretcher-bearer, on ten occasions carried badly wounded men on his back through particularly heavy artillery and machine-gun fire. Two of the wounded were hit a second time while on his back. Again, after a withdrawal over the river had been ordered, Private Poulter returned in full view of the enemy and carried back another man who had been left behind wounded. He bandaged forty men under fire and was seriously wounded when attempting another rescue in the face of the enemy. The town of Erquinghem-Lys, France erected a memorial to Private Poulter, next to the railway line. In 2005 the keys to the town were presented to the Duke of Wellington's (West Riding) Regiment.

Sergeant Lawrence Calvert

Lawrence Calvert was born in Hunslet but moved to live in Conisborough. He was educated at the Roman Road Board School and at the Cockburn School. On leaving school he was employed as a van boy by the Midland railway company at Leeds. He was 26 years old, and a sergeant in the 5th Battalion, The King's Own Yorkshire Light Infantry, when, on 12 September 1918 at the battle of Havrincourt, the following deed took place for which he was awarded the VC: for most conspicuous bravery and devotion to duty in attack when the success of the operation was rendered doubtful owing to severe enfilade machine-gun fire. Alone and single-handed Sergeant Calvert, rushing forward against the machine-gun team, bayoneted three and shot four. His valour and determination in capturing single-handed two machine guns and killing the crews thereof enabled the ultimate objective to be won. His personal gallantry inspired all ranks. He was also awarded the Military Medal and the Belgian Order of Leopold (with palm), in the grade of Chevalier.

As a fitting footnote to this chapter, Graham Wright, whose grandfather Reginald Wright was killed on 28 March 1918 but whose name was omitted from the Headingley memorial when it was originally unveiled in 1921, took steps to rectify the omission in September 2016. Thanks to Leeds City Council it was added in a ceremony on 2 April, 2017. Documents were provided as evidence that his grandfather should have been originally listed.

Private Wilfred Edwards

Edwards was born in Norwich but is buried in Wortley Cemetery, Leeds. He was 24 years old, and a private in the 7th Battalion, The King's Own Yorkshire Light Infantry, and was awarded the VC for his actions on 16 August 1917 at Langemarck, Belgium: when all the company officers were lost, Private Edwards, without hesitation and under heavy machine-gun and rifle fire from a strong concrete fort, dashed forward at great personal risk, bombed through the loopholes, surmounted the fort and waved to his company to advance. Three officers and thirty other ranks were taken prisoner by him in the fort. Later he did most valuable work as a runner and eventually guided most of the battalion out through very difficult ground. Throughout he set a splendid example and was utterly regardless of danger. Edwards was later commissioned a second lieutenant, in December 1917 and went on to serve in the Second World War as a major.

A German gas-attack outfit in the Royal Armouries Museum.

'Woodbine Willie'

Geoffrey Anketell Studdert Kennedy, MC (1883–1929) was an English Anglican priest and poet. He is best remembered by his nickname 'Woodbine Willie', earned during the war for lavishing Woodbine cigarettes along with spiritual aid on wounded and dying soldiers. He was born in Leeds in 1883, the seventh of nine children born to Jeanette Anketell and William Studdert Kennedy, vicar of St Mary's, Quarry Hill in Leeds. He was educated at Leeds Grammar School and Trinity College, Dublin, where he graduated in classics and divinity in 1904. Studdert Kennedy volunteered as a chaplain to the army on the Western Front; he was awarded the Military Cross at Messines Ridge when he ran into no man's land to help the wounded during an attack on the German frontline. A published poet, he authored *Rough Rhymes of a Padre* (1918), and *More Rough Rhymes* (1919). During the war he was an enthusiastic supporter of the British war machine: attached to a bayonet-training service, he toured with boxers and wrestlers to give morale-boosting speeches about the usefulness and efficacy of the bayonet.

The last man killed

Private George Edward Ellison (1878–11 November 1918) has the unfortunate honour to be the last British soldier to be killed in action in the First World War. He died at 9.30 a.m., a mere ninety minutes before the armistice was signed, while on a patrol outside Mons, Belgium. He was born and lived in Leeds, joining the army as a regular soldier only to leave in 1912 when he married Hannah Maria Burgan and became a coal miner. Just before the outbreak of war he was recalled to the army, joining the 5th Royal Irish Lancers. He fought at the battle of Mons in 1914, the first Ypres, Lens, Loos and Cambrai, among others. He is buried in the St Symphorien Military Cemetery, south-east of Mons.

Tragically, the Allies and Germany had signed the armistice ending the war six hours earlier but delayed its coming into effect until 11 a.m. so that the message could be conveyed to troops at the front. This delay cost Ellison his life. He was one of 11,000 casualties, dead and wounded, on that last day. By bizarre coincidence – because Mons was lost to the British at the very beginning of the war and regained at the very end – his grave faces that of John Parr, the first British soldier to be killed during the Great War.

8. LEEDS AND THE SECOND WORLD WAR

A mere twenty-one years after dancing in the streets to celebrate the end of the First World War, the people of Leeds were girding themselves up for another global conflict. In 1938 all households received a manual providing advice on respirators, refuge rooms and air raid procedures 'if ever there should be a war'. In 1941 Leeds City Council issued *After an Air Raid: Useful Information for the Citizen.* In January 1939 the West Riding National Service Committee was set up to compile a register of all those men and women eligible for armed service and auxiliary civilian units. Over 100,000 men were consequently signed up as well as 10,000 women in the various women's services. Unlike the previous war there were no local regiments and no Pals. More than 1,400 women were drafted into the Leeds transport department. Trams were imported from Hull and painted khaki, nets covered the windows, blackout masks the headlights. The 2,000 brick air-raid shelters in the city could hold 66,000 people.

More than 14,000 Anderson air-raid shelters were constructed to protect 300,000 Leeds citizens. Surface shelters were built in City Square, blast walls went up outside stores and

A late 1930s review of military and civil defence units in front to the half-finished Quarry Hill flats.

ARP (air-raid precautions) water tanks were positioned in the middle of roads. One and a half million sandbags were filled to protect public buildings. From November 1939 over 4 million ration books were issued in Leeds throughout the war. Children were targeted with 70,000 tins of 'National' dried milk while 12,500 bottles of cod liver oil and orange oil were given out every week. Mass evacuation of children was mobilized on 1 September when 18,250 children, 1,450 teachers and 1,350 volunteer helpers left the city for safer places in fifty-one special trains. Destinations included Retford, Lincoln, Doncaster, Worksop, Gainsborough, the Yorkshire Dales and Bramham Park. Next day a further forty-five trains took 8,167 mothers, pre-school children, pregnant women and people with sight impairment to other safer places. As in other places in the UK, most of the unaccompanied children came home after a month or two, homesick and missing their mothers.

Mr and Mrs Horace Fawcett relax in their air-raid shelter, October 1940 in Cardigan Avenue, Burley, actually a very comfortable reinforced coal cellar; the Leodis website tells that 'the Fawcetts were held up as a shining example of resourcefulness and ingenuity. When members of the ARP came to inspect this shelter, they found the walls neatly papered, electric lighting and a heater installed, chairs and a table, and pictures on the wall, with a cot for the baby in the corner. "It is a grand piece of work" was the comment of Cllr. HW Sellars, ARP chairman'. Many others just moaned about their shelters. (Courtesy of Leodis © Leeds Library & Information Services)

Paperwork and bureaucracy proliferated with ration books, coupons, manuals, identity cards and permits all churned out to support the war effort. The 18th Battalion West Riding Home Guard was raised with officers trained at Osterley Park by Spanish Civil War veterans. In West Yorkshire alone, seventy-three Home Guard battalions were raised: apart from the 18th, the 7th, 8th, 9th and 17th were also raised in Leeds along with the Aire & Calder Navigation Company and the 16th West Riding (17 GPO) Battalion. Fifteen thousand men and 2,000 women were called up to these Home Guard or Civil Defence units. The War Office dubbed these women 'Army Followers', clearly oblivious to the historical connotations. The two battalions in Leeds – one south and one north of the river – did valuable clerical and catering work. The men, meanwhile, manned anti-aircraft guns at Adel and Knostrop, guarded German POWs, manned roadblocks and wielded 3-inch smooth-bore Smith guns – which had to be overturned before they were in the firing position.

They also had Spigot mortars – anti-personnel and anti-tank weapons with a range of 450 yards. Apart from those in the city centre, units were stationed at Kirkstall Bridge, Silver Royd, Bramley, Farnley, Low Mills, City Station and Wellington Bridge.

There were two prisoner of war camps in Leeds. No. 244 was at Butcher Hill in Horsforth; No. 91 was at Post Hill Camp in Farnley. Butcher Hill prisoners produced a magazine, *Die Brücke* ('The Bridge'). It was named after a group of German expressionist

November 1939: getting the ration books ready.

Leeds Home Guard with a Spigot mortar.

POWs from Farnley road-building.

artists formed in Dresden in 1905, after which the Brücke Museum in Berlin was named. The prisoners were repatriated in 1947.

About 132 ARP posts sprang up with sixty training centres catering for over 7,000 ARP wardens. Leeds City Transport Department collected pans, railings, gates and irons to make armoured vehicles and guns. Refugees from the occupied Channel Islands and Belgium were welcomed to the city. Over a hundred private cars were converted into auxiliary ambulances to cope with civilian air-raid casualties although they were mainly used for ferrying injured soldiers to hospitals.

Gas attacks were a constant fear. January 1941 saw the establishment of a gas decontamination unit and there were disinfestations units at Beckett Street and Stanley Road. Leeds Co-op was at the forefront of entertainment provision with regular talks and variety performances in the Albion Street People's Hall. 1941 highlights included *Co-Op Capers* and *Albion Follies*. An ARP post operated from the basement of Leeds Town Hall and from 1942 a British Restaurant opened there, also known as the Civic Restaurant.

A local schoolmaster extolled the benefits of boys wearing shorts instead of trousers until age 16; apart from saving two coupons 'a well-made youth looks his best in shorts and stockings'. Indeed. Yorkshire's leading furriers – Direct of Vicar Lane – repurposed old furs, even 'old and shabby' ones.

Leeds women, of course, signed up for the Women's Land Army; by 1941 there were 20,000 volunteers working in the farms and fields nationwide; 80,000 by 1944. We know that fifty Leeds women worked at Thurnham Hall, East Dereham in Norfolk for the duration.

Winston Churchill visited Leeds on Saturday 16 May 1942; he spent three hours in the city which, for security reasons, had two hours' notice of his coming. Despite this, 20,000 people congregated at the Town Hall to hear him speak.

Fund-raising was big business in Leeds. Ark Royal Week – HMS *Ark Royal* was the city's adopted ship – brought in over £9 million for a replacement when a German U-boat sank model # 1 in November 1941. Ark Royal Week ran from 30 January to 7 February 1942 with an initial objective of £5 million. The National Savings Scheme netted over £72 million; in July 1943 Wings for Victory Week raised £7.2 million; War Weapons Week brought in £3.5 million and Salute the Soldier over £6 million. Leeds was the first English city to host a War Weapons Week with the first initiative, to raise money for 250 bombers, in September 1940. During the Second World War the people of Horsforth raised all of the £241,000 required to build the corvette HMS *Aubretia*. In 2000 US President Bill Clinton acknowledged Horsforth's contribution to the war effort in a letter sent to MP Paul Truswell. The letter is now in the local museum. Burton's employees contributed handsomely to the cost of a Spitfire in 1940. After VE Day the city continued to raise funds: In June 1945 Youth Marches On was a five-day victory festival organized by the *Yorkshire Evening News* and the Standing Conference of Youth Organizations.

Leeds schoolchildren on the Town Hall steps during Wings for Victory week in July 1943.

Leeds war industries

A fascinating revelation was made during renovation of the Kirkstall Brewery buildings when it was discovered that a Second World War submarine engine was installed at the brewery as power back-up. This engine was one of a pair built in 1943 but was never actually installed in a submarine. The size of a Ford Transit van, it was sold in 1948 to the brewery and now resides at the Anson Engine Museum in Poynton, Cheshire and is currently being restored.

Sir George Cohen & Sons in Stanningley employed 14,500 to produce aircraft, mainly Avro Ansons, along with other aeronautical engineering projects. There was another Avro plant at Yeadon producing components for Blackburn aircraft along with Tate's, Hudswell, Clarke & Co., Appleyards and Thomas Green & Co. producing Skua fighter dive-bombers for the Royal Navy, Firebrand torpedo planes, and twin-engine Botha bombers. Hudswell, Clarke & Co. also produced locomotives for the War Department, most famously Austerity Class locos. At the Wellington Street factory of Fairbairn, Lawson, Combe, Barbour Ltd. women workers bored two-pounder gun barrels.

Charles H. Roe Ltd.

As noted, cars became ambulances; for example, a 1935 Vauxhall 20 saloon was converted by Charles H. Roe Ltd., at Cross Gates Carriage works in Austhorpe Road. Charles Roe

Women working on Avro Anson engines at George Cohen & Sons.

Hudswell, Clarke & Co. Austerity Class locomotive.

converted the chassis of hundreds of private cars to ambulances and mobile canteens. But that was not all: they also turned out utility double-decker and single-decker buses to Ministry of Supply specifications that were destined for all over the country as well as various military utility vehicles that included mobile map-printing wagons and articulated trailer kitchens. 14,826 accumulator trolleys – trundled out onto runways to start aircraft engines – were also manufactured.

Vickers Armstrong

Vickers set up a factory in Leeds that focused on light and medium guns. By the end of the war it had produced nearly 9,000 pieces of ordnance for the British Army. Nationally the company produced two-thirds of the British Army's field artillery during the period and was also responsible for manufacturing the famous Vickers machine gun, which had been in production since the First World War. By 1940 tanks were lumbering off the production lines with Cruisers, Valentines and Matildas prominent.

ROF Barnbow

Barnbow manufactured guns for the army and navy and employed 3,000 workers, more than 2,000 of whom were women; women were actually conscripted into working from 1941 to keep the guns and ammunition coming. As we have seen, Barnbow Royal Ordnance Factory opened in 1915 and employed 17,000 people at its height, manufacturing munitions in the First World War. The factory was closed in the 1930s and the buildings were demolished. A new Barnbow Royal Ordnance Factory was built on a 60-acre site at Cross Gates at the beginning of the Second World War. At first it produced gun barrels and other gun parts, installing gun barrels on American Sherman tanks. From that it graduated into total tank production: first was the Centurion with more than 2,000 produced up until 1959.

ROF Thorp Arch (Filling Factory No. 9)

At the nearby Thorp Arch factory, hundreds of women were employed in repetitive and dangerous cartridge filling. Thorp Arch opened in July 1941. It produced munitions for the army, the Royal Navy and the Royal Air Force in 619 buildings, producing light and medium-gun ammunition, heavy ammunition, landmines and trench-mortar ammunition for the army; medium and large bombs for the RAF; and 20mm and other small-arms ammunition for all three services. Some of these were produced in the millions and hundreds of millions of items.

In 1943 Oxley's Mineral Water Company began producing Coca-Cola from a special concentrate when American troops arrived in the area. Greenwood & Batley moved into munitions manufacture, as did Mann's factory in Hunslet while John Fowler Engineering Co., also in Hunslet, a coachmaker, went over to making tanks and other combat vehicles.

Girls from West Leeds High School picking potatoes – picking for victory.

Burton's

As in the first war, Burton's was quick to adapt to the tailoring needs of the nation with a rapid conversion to the production of greatcoats and battledress. Overall, Burton's produced 13.6 million garments for all three services, 25 per cent of the total UK war manufacturing in this area. At the end of the war Montague Burton was one of the chief suppliers of demob suits, comprising jacket, trousers, waistcoat, shirt and underwear. This is the derivation of the phrase 'the full Monty'. Burton's suits may have lacked frills but they retained the keynote quality customers had come to expect from a Burton suit. By the end of the war, Burton was probably clothing around 20 per cent of British men. Legend has it that there was an RAF office over a Burton's shop somewhere, where servicemen would sit exams. Failing candidates were said to have 'gone for a Burton'.

Joseph Watson & Sons Ltd – Soapy Joe's

Joseph Watson & Sons Ltd. – Soapy Joe's – had its soap factory in Whitehall Road. Unlikely as it at first may seem, this soap manufacturer largely turned its hand away from soaps (which were rationed) to the manufacture of hand grenades, rifle grenades and anti-tank grenades, bomb tail units and valve bodies for various bombs. Glycerine, of course, was used in the production of TNT, with glycerine a byproduct of the soap-making process. Joseph Watson with his expertise was called upon assist the government in the establishment of national munitions factories and in particular the No. 1 National Shell Filling Factory at Barnbow.

John Waddington

When we think of the Leeds firm Waddingtons, images of 'Monopoly' spring to mind. But Waddingtons had a far more diverse range of products than the iconic board game and decks of cards might suggest. The Great War saw a boom in the demand for playing cards which Waddingtons helped to meet. In 1941, the British Secret Service (MI9) commissioned the company to produce a special edition of 'Monopoly' for Second World War prisoners of war held by the Germans. Secreted inside these sets were maps, compasses, real foreign currency and other objects essential for a successful escape. The games were distributed to camp escape committees by the International Red Cross. The escape and evasion maps, which also went in decks of playing cards, were printed on Bemberg silk (rayon) or on mulberry paper. Churchill himself encouraged an increase in production of cards to boost morale at home and abroad. The company also produced cartridge casings for ICI metals.

Leeds industry and business catered for every aspect of combat life in every theatre of war by all three services. Here is just a small selection of the fruits of Leeds's manufacturing output in aid of the war effort:

75,000 RAF greatcoats
90,000 duffle coats
700,000 drill shorts (khaki and green)
50,000 anti-mosquito skirts
50,000 snow suits
58 million cartridge bags
1.45 million labels for water purifying bags for jungle use
1.5 million flashes of tartan cloth
600,000 POW flashes
5,000 jungle epaulettes for nurses
120,000 insignia for USAAF flying personnel
1 million flags
50,000 pyjama suits
100,000 toe covers (mountain and snow)

400 6-pdr anti-tank guns
870 locomotives
143,000 hand grenades
250,000 binoculars and other optical instruments

900 million .303 inch cartridges

726 Lancaster bombers

3,920 Ansons and spares for 1,000 more

1,560 tanks

On 13 May 1945 over 2,000 people participated in a victory parade of auxiliary units through the city centre. Ex-prisoners of war were treated to a reception in Roundhay Park. The *Yorkshire Post* had run a POW club during the war, sending out food parcels and cigarettes to the camps: at the end of the war 20,000 members met at twenty-three centres while those who had been in Far East camps each received £5 from the POW fund.

Leeds regiments in the Second World War

69th Field Regiment, 49th (West Riding) Infantry Division

In 1939, the 69th Field Regiment, as part of the 49th (West Riding) Infantry Division formed a second-line regiment at Bramley, Leeds – the 121st Field Regiment RA (TA) which served in Iceland for two years. The 121st was posted to Iraq in 1941, fought with the British Eighth Army in the North Africa campaign and the American Fifth Army in the Italian campaign before returning to the United Kingdom to join the Normandy invasion as a medium regiment with 5.5-inch gun-howitzers at the battle for Caen, the battle for Le Havre in September 1944 (Operation Astonia) and the liberation of Arnhem in 1945.

Yorkshire Hussars

In September 1939 the Hussars remained in their squadron HQ towns in case they were required to keep order following German bombing raids. Later they were at Malton as part of 5th Cavalry Brigade with the Yorkshire Dragoons and Sherwood Rangers. They were then moved to Market Rasen in Lincolnshire and there formed the 1st Cavalry Division with the 4th and 6th brigades.

The division was posted to Palestine in January 1940 and in 1941 the Yorkshire Hussars were attached to the 6th Cavalry Brigade which later became 8th Armoured Brigade when they were then attached to the Staffordshire Yeomanry and the Scots Greys. The regiment converted to armour in October 1941 and trained on Stuart tanks. They were moved again, into the 9th Armoured Brigade with the Wiltshire and Warwickshire yeomanries. In March 1942 they found themselves in Cyprus, armed with Cruiser Mk III tanks and Valentines and now known as the Armoured Striking Force. In January 1943 they sailed to Egypt and were trained on Shermans and Crusader Mk IVs with further training on 75mm guns and desert tactics for the North Africa campaign.

That November the Yorkshire Hussars sailed from Alexandria back to the UK, arriving at Gourock on 12 December. They converted to an infantry reconnaissance regiment and were placed at first with the 50th (Northumbrian) Infantry Division, then under the command of 61st (South Midland) Infantry Division. From April to August the regiment was split into squadrons and put in charge of the D-Day embarkation camps in Sussex. A Squadron remained in the operational role. In August the regiment was reunited again to become a reconnaissance holding unit for refresher training and drafting of wounded reconnaissance personnel. In June 1945 the Hussars re-organized as a light armoured regiment with Churchill tanks.

45th & 51st (Leeds Rifles) Royal Tank Corps (TA) & 66th (Leeds Rifles) AA Regiment

A. J. Podmore, MBE, TD explains the situation regarding the Leeds Rifles immediately before the outbreak war:

> In 1936 the 8th (Leeds Rifles) Battalion was converted to Anti-Aircraft artillery. In 1938 the 7th (Leeds Rifles) Battalion was converted to the armoured rôle, and redesignated '45th (Leeds Rifles) Royal Tank Corps (TA)' (45 RTR). In early 1939 the Territorial Army was doubled in size requiring that existing units each raised 'duplicate units'. This resulted in 'A' Squadron of 45 RTR, at Morley, expanding to become a second regiment – '51st (Leeds Rifles) Royal Tank Regiment (TA)'. Both units adopted the badges of the Royal Tank Regiment retaining the Leeds Rifles' colours on their uniform shoulder-strap flashes. Both tank regiments served as such during the Second World War.

The 66th (Leeds Rifles) AA Regiment mobilized and became part of 31st AA Group which transferred to a new 7th Anti-Aircraft Division forming to defend north-east England. The 45th (Leeds Rifles) RTR formed part of 24th Army Tank Brigade (later 24th Armoured Brigade), a second-line territoral formation in Northern Command serving with the Oldham TA regiments, 41 RTR and its duplicate, 47 RTR. The duplicate Leeds battalion, 51 RTR, was in the 25th Army Tank Brigade, also in Northern Command, alongside the Newcastle TA regiment, 43 RTR, and its duplicate 49 RTR.

The 45th fought bravely at El Alamein, but was subsequently disbanded to provide battle replacement crews, having suffered high casualties. The regiment lost ten tanks; eleven men were killed or died of wounds with ten missing believed dead, and thirty-four wounded, mainly from mines and shell fire. The Lord Mayor of Leeds sent a message of congratulations to the 45th (Leeds Rifles) RTR.

The first years of the Second World War for the 51st Battalion Royal Tank Regiment were spent either in training for their new armoured role or in Home Defence duties in

Northumberland. In January 1943, disguised as gunners to fox any enemy intelligence operations, they were in action in North Africa under the command of British First Army in the Tunisian campaign. On 7–8 April the 51st RTR supported IX Corps at Fondouk Pass. The 128th Brigade of 46th Infantry Division crossed the Wadi Marguellil during the night and at 5.30 a.m. on 8 April began its main attack, supported by C Squadron 51st RTR, and by noon had taken its objective. The regiment ended the campaign in Army Reserve.

The brigade, including the 51st RTR, remained in Algeria, training for almost a year, before they were called up for the Italian campaign. The 51st RTR embarked on 16 April 1944 and landed at Naples, where it was equipped with Churchill tanks, Shermans and Stuarts. They advanced to Lucera, near Foggia, to join the 1st Canadian Division. On 12 May, the 51st crossed the River Gari and joined up with 3rd Canadian Infantry Brigade, before the successful attack on the Adolf Hitler Line. In the final attack on the line on 23 May 1944, the battalion, without B Squadron which had suffered heavy losses in a previous engagement, supported the Canadians in an attack on the left of the line.

An anti-aircraft battery in Leeds, 1941.

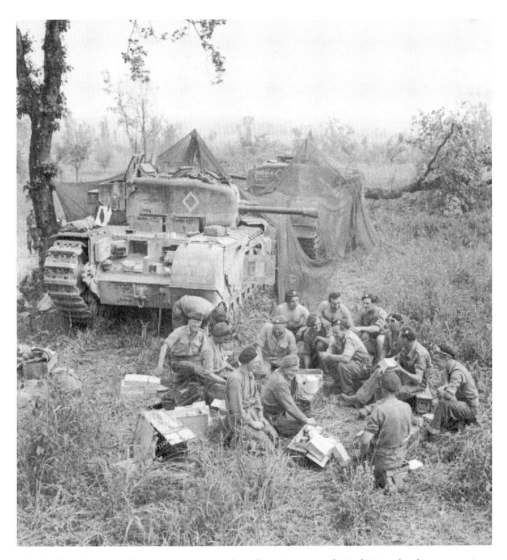

Churchill tank crews of HQ Troop, 51st Royal Tank Regiment, 25th Tank Brigade, share out rations near their camouflaged vehicles before going into action in support of 1st Canadian Division, Italy, May 1944 (Photo Johnson, Sgt., No. 2 Army Film & Photographic Unit 17 May 1944)

At 6 a.m. on 23 May, behind a barrage, the tanks and infantry advanced; however the 51st sustained many casualties – both tanks and men – in achieving their objective. After this the battalion parted company with the Canadians and continued to advance, rolling back the enemy line for another month before a break from front-line action. The Canadian Division later decorated the unit with the emblem of the Canadian Maple Leaf which is, to this day, worn as part of regimental dress.

In January 1945 the 51st RTR was converted to specialized armour. B Squadron was issued with Crab Mk II flail tanks, while A and C squadrons took possession of thirty-two Churchill Crocodile flame-throwing tanks. Their last action of the war was as part of the 25th Armoured Assault Brigade at the crossing of the Senio on 9 April 1945. The 51st RTR was attached to the 2nd New Zealand and 8th Indian divisions deploying their Crocodile flame-throwers to good effect.

The 66th (Leeds Rifles) AA Regiment was part of 31st AA Brigade during the early years of the war. The 197th Battery left the regiment, and later the 296th Battery joined from the 96th AA Regiment at Castleford. In the summer of 1940 the 66th was designated a heavy AA regiment and that September was assigned to the Orkneys and Shetland Defence Force, mainly guarding the naval base at Scapa Flow. In June 1941 the 66th returned to England to join the 62nd AA Brigade in the 10th Anti-Aircraft Division covering Yorkshire. In May 1942 the regiment was posted to India where it served in the 1st and 2nd Indian AA brigades before moving to Burma as part of the 9th AA Brigade. During 1943 the regiment served in the Manipur Road sector and stayed in the same areas, as part of the 3rd Indian AA Brigade.

Flight Sergeant Arthur Louis Aaron VC, DFM (Posthumous)

Arthur Aaron was born in Leeds, and educated at Roundhay School and Leeds School of Architecture. In 1939 he joined the Air Training Corps squadron at Leeds University and trained as a pilot in the United States at No. 1 British Flying Training School (BFTS) at Terrell, Texas. Aaron returned to England to train at an Operation Conversion Unit before he joined No. 218 'Gold Coast' Squadron, flying Short Stirling heavy bombers from RAF Downham Market. This is his story, as told by the Air Ministry, 5 November 1943 in the official citation for his VC:

> On the night of 12 August 1943, Flight Sergeant Aaron [aged 21] was captain and pilot of a Stirling aircraft detailed to attack Turin. When approaching to attack, the bomber received devastating bursts of fire from an enemy fighter. Three engines were hit, the windscreen shattered, the front and rear turrets put out of action and the elevator control damaged, causing the aircraft to become unstable and difficult to control. The navigator was killed and other members of the crew were wounded.
>
> A bullet struck Aaron in the face, breaking his jaw and tearing away part of his face. He was also wounded in the lung and his right arm was rendered useless. As he fell forward over the control column, the aircraft dived several thousand feet. Control was regained by the flight engineer at 3,000 feet. Unable to speak, Aaron urged the bomb aimer by signs to take over the controls. Course was then set southwards in an endeavour to fly the crippled bomber, with one engine out of action, to Sicily or North Africa.
>
> Flight Sergeant Aaron was assisted to the rear of the aircraft and treated with morphia. After resting for some time he rallied and, mindful of his responsibility

as the captain of the aircraft, insisted on returning to the cockpit, where he was lifted into his seat and had his feet placed on the rudder bar. Twice he made determined attempts to take control and hold the aircraft to its course but his weakness was evident and with difficulty he was persuaded to desist. Though in great pain and suffering from exhaustion, he continued to help by writing directions with his left hand.

Five hours after leaving the target area, fuel began to run low, but soon afterwards the flare path at Bone airfield was sighted. Aaron summoned his failing strength to direct the bomb aimer in the hazardous task of landing the damaged aircraft in the darkness with undercarriage retracted. Four attempts were made under his direction; at the fifth Flight Sergeant Aaron was so near to collapsing that he had to be restrained by the crew and the landing was completed by the bomb aimer.

Nine hours after landing, Flight Sergeant Aaron died from exhaustion. Had he been content, when grievously wounded, to lie still and conserve his failing strength, he would probably have recovered, but he saw it as his duty to exert himself to the utmost, if necessary with his last breath, to ensure that his aircraft and crew did not fall into enemy hands. In appalling conditions he showed the greatest qualities of courage, determination and leadership and, though wounded and dying, he set an example of devotion to duty which has seldom been equalled and never surpassed.

He had flown ninety operational flying hours in nineteen sorties. He was also posthumously awarded the Distinguished Flying Medal for a separate action of bravery. A statue to Arthur is sited close to the West Yorkshire Playhouse at the start of the Headrow.

The Leeds Blitz

Throughout the war seventy-seven Leeds people were killed and 197 buildings were destroyed with 7,623 damaged, and subsequently repaired, in nine raids and eighty-seven air-raid alerts. There were twenty-four major fires. Leeds firefighters were comparatively under-worked and sent crews to deal with fires in London, Liverpool, York, Coventry, Sheffield, Birmingham and Hull where the bombing was, York apart, much heavier.

On 2 September 1940, between 3,000 and 4,000 incendiaries and fourteen high-explosive bombs were dropped on the city. 14/15 March 1941 saw Leeds's most devastating raid, the so-called 'Quarter Blitz' after the tonnage of bombs dropped. In Morley there was damage to property in Spenslea Grove, Homefield Avenue and Model Road. Casualties: one fatal, four injured. In the city centre incendiaries fell on Aire Street; the Town Hall and City Museum were badly damaged, partially destroying the Law Library in the Town Hall, and some of the Egyptology collection in the museum. Kirkstall power station was a target. The Hepworth Arcade and the streets around

A bomb-damaged Marsh Lane station on 1 September 1940.

Water Lane were alight. By midnight Mill Hill Chapel, the Royal Exchange Building, Denby & Spink's furniture store and the Yorkshire Post building had been hit. These were followed by bombs at Gipton, Headingley, Woodhouse and Roundhay roads. There was further damage at Fairbairn Lawson's, Greenwood & Batleys, Wellington Street, Wellington Road goods yard and Central and City stations. The Infirmary, Town Hall, City Museum, Kirkgate market, St Peter's School, Park Square, Hotel Metropole and Quarry Hill flats were also hit.

Twenty-five tons of bombs fell on Leeds during the raid, a quarter of the 100 tons used as the threshold to qualify as a 'major raid'. Bad enough, but to put it into perspective, by comparison, that same night in Glasgow 203 aircraft dropped 231 tons of high explosives, and 1,650 incendiaries , while in Sheffield 117 aircraft dropped 83 tons of high explosives and 328 incendiaries. The bombers over Leeds were probably Junkers Ju 88s and Dornier Do 17s if those shot down in other parts of Yorkshire that night are anything to go by.

Above: Some serious bomb damage in Easterly Road on 2 September 1940.

Below: How the Luftwaffe neatly converted this semi into a detached house on 22 September 1941 in a cul-de-sac off Cliff Road. (Courtesy of Leodis © Leeds Library & Information Services)

Washing day in East Grove Street, Burmantofts, probably a Monday. (Courtesy of Leodis © Marc Riboud 1954 and Leeds Library & Information Services)

This is an extract from the *West Yorkshire Archive Service* report:

Just after 9 o'clock on the evening of the Friday 14th March, Air Raid Sirens across the City sounded the 'alert'. Fire watchers on the roof of the Turner Tanning Machinery Company in Bramley reported planes flying from the East to the North West at 9.15pm and shortly after that the City was hit repeatedly and was quickly ablaze ... 65 people including 8 children died that night and a further 258 were injured. Despite the entrance to the casualty department being hit by a bomb, the Leeds General Infirmary Air Raid In-Patients book shows that 59 people were admitted in the early hours of the 15th March with injuries ranging from burns to shock. Over 4000 Wardens and 1,800 fire crew were on hand to assist the public. Fire services were called out to 116 fires caused by enemy action through the night.

The Oak Road Congregational Church was hit and partially destroyed in October 1941. Kirkstall Forge was bombed on the night of 27/28 August 1942: five workers died when the bar-drawing shop and the rear-axle casing shop were hit. The Forge was camouflaged and had its own Home Guard Unit to defend it from ground attack or sabotage.

Hitler coming down Briggate, but not how he would have chosen it.

VJ Day, 15 August 1945 outside the Town Hall.

Leeds wartime Meals on Wheels delivered by the WVS. Over two million meals are still delivered daily to the elderly and infirm.

The 31st (North Midland) Anti-Aircraft Brigade provided anti-aircraft defence of West Yorkshire, and throughout the war Leeds obviously had anti-aircraft guns positioned throughout the city. The Leeds Anti-Bomb School was based at Sweet Street. RAF Marston Moor and RAF Church Fenton were the closest airfields to Leeds and provided defence for the city. At Church Fenton Group Captain Leonard Cheshire was the station commander in 1943; Clark Gable was stationed at the airfield before being posted to RAF Polebrook. RAF Marston Moor was originally called RAF Tockwith, but confusion with RAF Topcliffe lead to a prudent name change. HMS *Ceres* in Wetherby, an inland naval base, was nearby.

RAF Yeadon & the Avro shadow factory

The aerodrome, now the Leeds Bradford Airport, opened as the Leeds and Bradford Municipal Aerodrome, Yeadon Aerodrome, on 17 October 1931 and was operated by the Yorkshire Aeroplane Club for Leeds and Bradford corporations. Scheduled flights began in 1935 with a service by North Eastern Airways from Heston Aerodrome in London to Cramlington at Newcastle upon Tyne, later extended to Edinburgh's Turnhouse. Civil aviation was, of course, suspended in 1939.

In 1942 Avro built a new factory to produce military aircraft just to the north of the aerodrome; around 5,515 aircraft were produced and delivered from Yeadon during the war including Ansons (over 4,500), Bristol Blenheims (250), Lancasters (695), Yorks (45) and Lincolns (25).

Two new runways, taxiways and extra hangars made Yeadon an important site for military aircraft test-flying. The Avro factory was camouflaged, replicating the original field pattern, apparently carried out by people in the film industry, and had dummy cows placed on the roof of the factory to fool German airmen into thinking that it was just a field of cattle beneath them. There were also imitation farm buildings, stone walls and a duck pond all placed around the factory. Hedges and bushes made out of fabric were periodically changed to match the changing colours of the seasons. Dummy animals were moved around daily to mimic activity. It all obviously worked because enemy bombers never detected the factory.

At its height during the war there was a staff of more than 17,500 people employed at Avro Yeadon. It was one of twenty-six 'shadow factories', and also the largest in Europe with a site of around thirty-four acres. The factory operated round the clock with workers on shift sixty-nine hours a week on a three-day followed by a three-night basis. Many of the workers were female, local girls supplemented by large numbers bussed in from all over West Yorkshire. The Ministry of Aircraft Production (MAP) built temporary homes or provided accommodation, for example, on the Westfield Estate in Yeadon and Greenbanks at Horsforth, for workers who lived at a distance from the Avro assembly plant.

British shadow factories came about from the government Shadow Scheme of 1935 in an attempt to meet the urgent need for aircraft using technology from the motor industry. The term 'shadow' has nothing to do with secrecy, but describes the skilled motor industry staff shadowing their own motor industry operations.

609 Squadron

The 609 (West Riding) Squadron was formed and based at RAF Yeadon from 10 February 1936 until 27 August 1939 as a day bomber unit of the Auxiliary Air Force; it was then posted to Catterick; the squadron returned in 1946 with Mosquito Mk XXX aircraft. It took receipt of Hawker Hart light bombers in June 1936, soon replaced in December 1937 by Hawker Hinds before the squadron was redesignated a fighter unit on 8 December 1938. There were no fighters, though, until the arrival of Spitfire Mk 1s at the end of August 1939, on the eve of the war. The squadron was still staffed by part-time civilians. Fairey Battle light bombers were used as training aircraft to convert pilots from the fixed undercarriage biplane Hinds to the Spitfire with its retractable undercarriage.

After defensive duties in the north, No. 609 moved to RAF Northolt in May 1940 and patrolled over Dunkirk as part of Operation Dynamo to cover the evacuation of the BEF. Around this period, one third of the squadron's pilots were lost over a period of three days. When 609 Squadron decamped to Catterick, Yeadon became a flying training school, bomber maintenance unit, and a scatter airfield. In January 1942 it was transferred to the Ministry of Aircraft Production when Avro then built their shadow factory. It was also used by Hawker Aircraft for development work on its Tornado design.

EPILOGUE: THE ROYAL ARMOURIES MUSEUM

There can be no more fitting an epilogue to Leeds's military heritage than the Royal Armouries Museum; this displays the National Collection of Arms and Armour and is also the National Fireams Centre. It forms one part of the Royal Armouries family of three museums, the others being the Tower of London and Fort Nelson, near Portsmouth.

Five galleries house 75,000 objects along with the Peace Gallery; the museum also features the Hall of Steel, a huge staircase 'whose walls are decorated with trophy displays composed of 2,500 objects reminiscent of the historical trophy displays erected by the Tower Armouries from the 17th century'. The archive holds 27,785 items and the library houses a 63,026-item collection. The gallery of most interest to us is 'War' with displays dedicated to Ancient and Medieval warfare, 17th and 18th centuries, and 19th and 20th centuries.

The Hall of Steel in all its splendour is the largest display ever amassed since the 17th century. Alexander the Great started it all off when he displayed what are believed to be Trojan arms from the Trojan War in the temple of Apollo at Ilium.

Rifles in the Hall of Steel.

A howitzer HE shell, the like of which would have been filled at Barnbow.

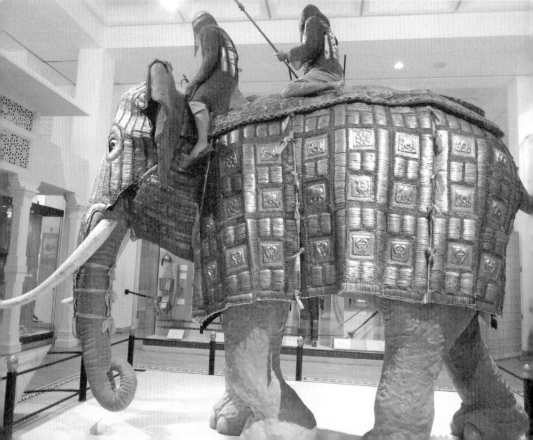

Above: British colonial tiger hunt.

Facing above: The magnificent Second World War panel of the West Riding Wood Carvers' Association; 70 members have painstakingly carved these 95 tableaux out of lime wood, taking about 100 hours over each. There is a similar but different panel for the First World War.

Facing below: Lamellar elephant armour from India around 1600 AD. This is a complete suit of elephant armour, the only example of such in any public collection in the world. It is made up of 8,450 separate iron plates interwoven with fabric and would have weighed about 160kg, making it easily the heaviest suit of armour in the world. It came with a pair of armour-piercing tusk swords.

Early 17th-century Indian Mughal heavy cavalryman.

SOURCES & FURTHER READING

1914 in Yorkshire, York Museums Trust York, 2014

Addyman, R. *A Leeds Family in the Second World War*, Leeds, 2010

Addyman, R. *The Leeds Rifles: A Concise Regimental History*, Leeds, 2010

Addyman, R. *Leeds and the Second World War Experience*, Leeds, 2008

Addyman, R. *The 45th (Leeds Rifles) Royal Tank Regiment in the Second World War*, Leeds, 2006

Beckett, A. F. W. *Britain's Part-Time Soldiers: The Amateur Military Tradition 1558–1945*, Barnsley, 2011

Beckett, A.F.W. *Riflemen Form: A Study of the Rifle Volunteer Movement 1859–1908*, Barnsley, 2007

Belton, B. *War Hammers: The Story of West Ham United During the First World War*, Stroud, 2006

Bennett, W. *Absent-Minded Beggars: Yeomanry and Volunteers in the Boer War*, Barnsley, 1999

Beresford, M. W. 'Leeds in 1628', *Northern History* X, 1975

Binns, J. *Yorkshire in the Civil Wars*, Pickering, 2004

Birch, L. *Remembering the Barnbow Tragedy: 100 Years Ago Today.* Local and Family History, Leeds Central Library, https://secretlibraryleeds.net/tag/barnbow/

Boud, R. C. *The Great Exodus: The Evacuation of Leeds Schoolchildren 1939–1945*, Leeds, 1999

Brown. C. *Ilkley and the Great War*, Stroud, 2014

Boyle, W. *History of the 2nd West Yorkshire Royal Engineers Volunteers and Its Successors*, Leeds, 1936

Chrystal, P. *Central Leeds through Time*, Stroud, 2017

Chrystal, P. *Women at War in Ancient Greece & Rome*, Barnsley, 2017

Chrystal. P. *Leeds in 50 Buildings*, Stroud, 2016

Chrystal. P. *Tadcaster through Time*, Stroud, 2016

Chrystal, P. *A–Z of York History*, Stroud, 2015

Clarendon, Edward Hyde, earl of & Mackray, W. D. (ed). *The History of the Rebellion and Civil Wars in England*, 6 vols, Oxford, 1888

Cocroft, W. D. *Dangerous Energy: The Archaeology of Gunpowder and Military Explosives Manufacture*, Swindon, 2000

Cooke, D. *Yorkshire Sieges of the Civil War*, Barnsley, 2011

Cooke, D. *The Civil War in Yorkshire*, Barnsley, 2004

Cooke, D. *The Forgotten Battle: The Battle of Adwalton Moor, 30th June 1643*, Battlefield Press, 1996

Douglas, J. (ed) *British Labour and the Russian Revolution: The Leeds Convention of 1917*, Nottingham, 2017

Farrar, J. W. *Leeds to Persia: The Autobiography of J. W. Farrar*. Amazon ed., 2014

Gummer, R.H. *How the Shells were Filled: The Story of Barnbow, Told Now for the First Time*, Leeds, 1919

Hagerty, J. M. *Leeds at War 1914–18, 1939–45*, Wakefield, 1981

Hargrave, E. 'The Early Leeds Volunteers', *Thoresby Society* 28, 1928, 255-284

Hargrave, E. 'The Gentlemen Volunteer Cavalry 1797', *Thoresby Society* 27, 1928, 284-291

Hargrave, E. 'Leeds Volunteers 1803–1808', *Thoresby Society* 28, 1928, 284-291

Hargrave, E. 'Leeds Local Militia 1808–1814', *Thoresby Society* 27, 1928, 313-319

Hay, I. *ROF: The Story of the Royal Ordnance Factories: 1939–48*, London, 1949

Hopper, A. J. 'The Clubmen of the West Riding of Yorkshire During the First Civil War', *Northern History* XXXVI, 2000

Hopper, A. J. 'The Extent of Support for Parliament in Yorkshire', PhD diss., University of York, 1999

Imperial War Museum (4 April 2005), 'Building Flying Boats by Flora Lion', *BBC History*, retrieved 10 May 2017

http://www.bbc.co.uk/history/trail/wars_conflict/art/art_daily_life_03.shtml

https://arts.leeds.ac.uk/legaciesofwar/resources/links/

https://arts.leeds.ac.uk/legaciesofwar/themes/yorkshire-and-the-great-war/

Johnson, D. *Adwalton Moor 1643: The Battle That Changed a War*, Pickering, 2003

Jones. J. 'The War in the North: The Northern Parliamentary Party in the English Civil War 1642–1645' PhD diss., University of Ontario, 1991

Lackey, C. *Quality Pays: The Story of Joshua Tetley & Son*, Ascot, 1985

'Leeds to Victory 1939–45', *Yorkshire Evening News*, Leeds, 1946

Litchfield, N. E. H. *The Volunteer Artillery 1859–1908*, Nottingham, 1982

Lynch, T. *Voices of the First World War: Yorkshire's War*, Stroud 2014

Middlebrook, M. *The First Day on the Somme*, London, 1971

Mitchell, J. C. Lt.-Col, TD. 'The West Riding Regiment Royal Artillery (Territorials)', www.yorkshirevolunteers.org.uk/wrarty.htm, 2000

Mitchinson, K. W. *Pioneer Battalions in the Great War: Organized and Intelligent Labour*, Barnsley, 2014

Moore, L. *Leeds: Remembering 1914–18*, Stroud, 2015

Morris, P. M. 'Leeds and the Amateur Military Tradition: The Leeds Rifles and their Antecedents c. 1859–1918', PhD diss., University of Leeds School of History, September 1983

Morris, Ruth & Morris, Pamela. *Their Names Live For Evermore: The Sacrifice of Leeds Jewish Servicemen in the Great War 1914–1919*, 2013

The National Roll of the Great War 1914–1918: Leeds Section VIII, Uckfield, 2001

Newman, P. R. 'The Royalist Armies in Northern England 1642–1645' 2 vols, DPhil diss., University of York, 1978

Podmore, A. J. MBE, TD, 'The Award of the Croix de Guerre avec Palme en Bronze: An extract from The Leeds Rifles 1859–1993 produced for Bligny Sunday, July 16th 2000', www.yorkshirevolunteers.org.uk/awardcroixdeguerre.htm

Robinson, J. R. *The Battle of Adwalton Moor*, 1877

Routledge, N. W. *History of the Royal Regiment of Artillery: Anti-Aircraft Artillery 1914–55*, London, 1994

Scott, W. H. *Leeds in the Great War, 1914–1918. A book of remembrance*, Uckfield, 1923

Seddon, W. 'The Leeds Volunteer Artillery', www.yorkshirevolunteers.org.uk/wrarty.htm, 2000

Sheehan, J. *Harrogate Terriers*, Barnsley 2017

Stowe, D. 'Legacies of War: The University of Leeds War Memorial', *Stand To, Journal of the Western Front Association* 105, 2016

Taylor, Elliot & Alston, Barney. *Up The Hammers!: The West Ham Battalion in the Great War 1914–18*, 2012

Tyler, T. E. & Tyler, G. E. B. *Leeds to Rangoon and Back: With the 66th Leeds Rifles Heavy Anti-Aircraft Regiment (TA) and 5th Indian Light Anti-Aircraft Regiment*, Ingelton, 2008

Wade, S. *Leeds in the Great War*, Barnsley, 2016

Walker, H. *Recollections: Sixty Years Ago and Onward* 2nd ed., Leeds, 1930

Westlake, R. *Tracing the Rifle Volunteers: A Guide for Military and Family Historian*, Barnsley, 2010

White, S. 'Soviets in Britain: The Leeds Convention of 1917', www.cambridge.org/core/services/aop-cambridge-core/content/view/

Wilcocks, R. *Stories from the War Hospital*, Leeds, 2014

Wyatt, T. J. 'The Leeds Volunteer Artillery 1947–1971', www.yorkshirevolunteers.org.uk/wrarty.htm, 1971

Wyrall, E. *The West Yorkshire Regiment 1914–1918*. London, 1923

Ziegler, F. *The Story of 609 Squadron: Under the White Rose*, London, 1971

ACKNOWLEDGEMENTS

Thanks to David Skillen, Towton Battlefield Society for the re-enactment images; John Fawkes and britishbattles.com for the maps of the three civil war battles; David Biggins (david.biggins@angloboerwar.com); Sally Hughes, Assistant Librarian Manager, Local and Family History Library, Leeds Central Library for the Leodis images; Martin Edwards at www.roll-of-honour.com for the Leeds City Engineers Department Roll of Honour; St James's Hospital, Leeds, for the image of the workhouse graveyard; Keith Rowntree, Archive and Special Collections Libraries and Learning Innovation, Leeds Beckett University for the City of Leeds Training College 2nd Northern General Hospital images; and Nicola Pullan, Assistant Curator of Leeds and Social History, Leeds Museums and Galleries for allowing me to see the Leonora Cohen archive material at the Abbey House Museum, Kirkstall.

ABOUT THE AUTHOR

Paul Chrystal is the author of some seventy books published over the last decade, including recent publications on Leeds's architecture and history, and on conflict and warfare: *Leeds in 50 Buildings*, *Central Leeds Through Time*, *Wars and Battles of the Roman Republic*, *Roman Military Disasters* and *Women and War in Ancient Greece and Rome* (2017). He is a regular contributor to history magazines, local and national newspapers and has appeared on BBC Radio 4, BBC World Service and on BBC local radio throughout Yorkshire, and in Teesside and Manchester.